In good company

Sophie lives with her family on a farm just outside Orange in country New South Wales. She trained in print journalism at the University of Canberra and has over 20 years' experience as a features writer. She has been blogging at local-lovely.com since 2013 and now also teaches social media and content marketing to producers and small businesses via *My Open Kitchen* (podcast, e-course and workshops). With this and her previous book, *A Basket by the Door*, also published by Murdoch Books, Sophie continues to build her wonderful community of home cooks, brimming with friendship and kindness.

Sophie Hansen

In good company

Simple, generous recipes and ideas for get-togethers and good times

murdoch books

Sydney | London

Autumn

Winter

THE BEST OF TIMES

This book is my love letter to shared tables of good food. It came together over a year of travelling around the country visiting family and friends and taking over their kitchens to cook with and for them. We dragged tables into gardens and paddocks and set them up, we shared picnics on windswept headlands, we had cosy kitchen suppers and we barbecued lamb on the back of a boat (while I tried not to fall in with my camera while going in for the 'hero shot').

Ask anyone to tell you about the most memorable, meaningful meal of their life and I promise they won't give you a chronological playback of what they ate; they'll tell you about how that meal made them *feel*. They'll remember the candlelight and the smell of roses in the centre of the table. They'll talk about the moment everyone tasted that hot lemon pudding and how it was light and fresh, but warm and comforting at the same time. They'll remember the spontaneous game of celebrity head and how they hadn't laughed like that in ages, or how, on that stinking hot February evening, that big bowl of pasta served outside under fairy lights with a pitcher of tangy, delicious cocktails was like a balm.

There is so much that we can't control, but how we feed the people we love and show them that love through a table set with pretty flowers, candles, your best napkins and their favourite food? This is in our control and it's powerful stuff.

I write this, and the following pages, in celebration of conviviality. I hope this book will give you some ideas for gatherings to have at your own place soon, whether a lovely morning tea, or drinks and a 'chatter platter' next Friday night or a quiet supper in the back garden with the neighbours.

Ultimately, all of this is just about being together. It's about belonging, being looked after, looking after others in return and feeling like you are a part of something, even for just a night.

And I promise that if the food is tasty, the table has been set with a little care, the drinks are flowing and the music is playing, it will be the best of times. And don't we all need more of those?

Still not feeling up to it? Here are some more words of encouragement to get you over the line and onto the phone to organise a dinner this weekend...

My house is a mess and/or not fancy enough

Your friends aren't coming to peek into your cupboards or judge the pile of laundry on the bed. They are coming to see you – to share a meal, tell some stories and have a few wines at the end of the week. Unless you start drawing attention to it, the state of your house will hardly get noticed. Also, I bet it's not nearly as bad as you think it is. And finally, lighting is everything! Turn off the overhead lights, turn on the lamps and light candles – everything looks good in the right lighting.

I can't do fancy food

Great, because we don't want fancy food – that's what we save up and go to restaurants for! Your friends just want good, tasty food plonked in the middle of the table to share, with no rush or stress. I know people who feel so anxious about cooking, despite the fact that they really can cook. I think that's such a shame because it stops them from having friends over or enjoying it when they do. Also, embrace shortcuts: don't hesitate to use frozen pastry and/or buy a roasted chook from the shops, and instead of dessert just buy some yummy rocky road or put out a plate of beautiful fresh fruit. Keep it simple, make it feel special with lighting and flowers... and just do it!

I'm on a budget and it doesn't stretch to entertaining

Having people over shouldn't be stressful or expensive (and it really doesn't have to be). Honestly, a big bowl of pasta with some greens, followed by a plate of peaches and a bowl of chocolates to share is a beautiful and affordable meal. Cooking with the seasons is also much more affordable than forking out for imported figs in the middle of winter (please don't do that). And, when people offer to bring something, say yes! Delegating a few elements of the meal can take off the pressure, too.

My house isn't big enough for entertaining

I'm sure it is, but okay, let's go into the backyard, to the park or to the beach and have a picnic. We just want to catch up!

I can't face feeding all those kids!

I know, I know – it can be tricky when you have a few families over and dinner needs to please toddlers, teens and their parents all at once. I think the easiest thing is to forgo any ambitions of sophisticated dining and instead embrace the chaos. Get everyone round for an 'early dinner' and pick a serve-yourself crowd pleaser (for example, a barbecue, the burgers on page 238 or the porchetta on page 16). Put everything on a table outside, spread out picnic rugs and let everyone serve themselves and sit where they like.

I always get stuck on what to cook and how to put together a full menu

Well, you're in the right place because this book is broken down into seasonal chapters with menus for all kinds of occasions. And they're all easy and also delicious.

I just don't have time to clean the house, shop and cook

I know, it seems like a lot. But to your first point, please refer to my earlier answer about the state of your house. Also, as my mum always says, never apologise for your house – it just draws attention to any mess that might be lurking. And why are we apologising, anyway? (I need to heed this one more!) Plus, the vast majority of the menus in this book aren't very time consuming. And finally, I'd argue that the time you do put into making food to share with your friends is time well spent and you won't regret a second of it.

SPRING

These gentle spring days are for picnics in tall green grass with a thermos of stew, a big crunchy salad, a jar of biscuits and your picnic rug. Heaven.

Let go of perfection; as long as there's plenty of tasty food, good company and drinks to go around, that's all people want!

Shake off winter with a long spring lunch in the garden – no flies, no snakes and no stinking heat!

Spring serves up its fair share of chilly afternoons, but after a long winter cooped up, we're all busting to get outside for picnics and fresh air.

Feeding the masses

This is a great menu to serve when you're entertaining a few families and you need something that everyone will like, from five-year-olds to hollow-legged teens, their parents and everyone in between. Porchetta completely fits this bill, especially served with crusty torpedo rolls, salsa verde to cut through the pork fat, crunchy bits of crackling (which I promise will be the very first thing to go) and a mellow, crunchy slaw.

The entire meal can be prepared well in advance, so all you need to do on the day is slice the pork and put everything out for everyone to assemble for themselves.

My tips for feeding a crowd

Menus like this are perfect for doubling (or tripling) if you are feeding a crowd because the workload is still pretty light and all the prep is done in advance, so you aren't left with your kitchen looking like a bomb site after everyone leaves! If you have around 20 people coming over for dinner or lunch, here are a few steps you could take to make it easy and fun rather than stressful and expensive.

1. Double the recipes and don't forget to order the meat from your butcher at least a week in advance.
2. Accept offers of help. People are generally super happy to bring something and keen to feel useful so please say yes if people offer, or just ask! You could delegate the slaw to one or two friends, the salsa verde to another and the bread rolls to someone else.
3. Double the mousse recipe, or make things really easy for yourself and load up the freezer with a selection of fancy ice creams, and then keep a bit of nice home-made rocky road or Caramel popcorn with smashed pretzels (page 218) to bring out later on.
4. Set up a table outside (weather permitting) and make that your serving 'station' so people can come and help themselves. I usually put a big picnic rug out in the garden for the kids to sit on for dinner (we don't have a table to seat 20!).
5. When you're feeding that many, the porchetta rolls really come into their own because you can get away with just using napkins or paper plates, and avoid a scene of mass devastation in the sink with 20 sets of crockery and cutlery to wash!
6. Let go of any ideals of perfection. As long as there is plenty of hot, tasty food to eat, good company and drinks to go around, that's all people will remember.

MARINATED GREEN OLIVES *and feta*
PORCHETTA *rolls with* SALSA VERDE ❧ FENNEL, PARMESAN *and* APPLE SLAW
APRICOT MOUSSE

String up some fairy lights, load up your speaker with fun tunes and you're instantly on your way to a good night.

Fennel, parmesan and apple slaw

Thinly slice ½ white cabbage, 4 fennel bulbs and 3 green apples (I use a mandolin) and combine in a large bowl. Add ¼ cup (60 g) good-quality mayonnaise, 2 Tbsp dijon mustard, the juice of 1 lemon and ½ cup (45 g) grated parmesan cheese. Using your hands, mix everything together really well. Add 1 cup (125 g) toasted slivered almonds. Check the seasoning, add salt and pepper to taste and a little more mayonnaise if needed. Cover and keep in the fridge until serving. *Serves 8–10*

MARINATED GREEN OLIVES *and feta*

This is a really simple, delicious starter, especially when passed around with some sliced baguette or lavosh crackers. It's also great when you finely chop the olives and toss it through some warm pasta or pearl couscous.

SERVES 8–10 AS A STARTER
PREP TIME : 15 MINS ⚬ COOK TIME : 10 MINS

4 cups (500 g) pitted green olives
4 garlic cloves, each sliced into a few pieces
2 rosemary sprigs
Grated or sliced zest of 2 lemons
1/2 cup (125 ml) extra virgin olive oil
2 cups (260 g) crumbled feta cheese

Combine the olives, garlic, rosemary, lemon zest and olive oil in a frying pan. Cook over medium heat for about 10 minutes or until the oil is just simmering and the whole lot is smelling wonderful.

Remove the pan from the heat and set aside to cool for about 10 minutes (if the oil is too hot, the feta will melt and lose its shape).

Put the crumbled feta in a serving bowl. Pour the olive mixture over the top and gently mix everything together. Serve at room temperature with sliced baguette or lavosh crackers.

SALSA VERDE

I don't think you can go wrong when you put a bowl of salsa verde down next to pretty much any dish, especially one as rich as the porchetta. This brilliant green slurry of herbs, lemon juice and salt is always welcome. I usually prepare a double batch, keeping a jar in the fridge ready to pour over everything from soft-boiled eggs to Chicken potato salad (see page 127) or a tray of roasted vegetables.

MAKES ABOUT 2 CUPS (500 ML)
PREP TIME : 10 MINS ⚬ COOK TIME : NIL

4 cups soft herbs (see Note)
3 garlic cloves, peeled
6 anchovy fillets
2 Tbsp capers, rinsed
Juice of 2 lemons, or to taste
1/3 cup (80 ml) extra virgin olive oil

Combine all the ingredients in a mortar and pestle or food processor and pound or pulse to combine. Taste and add more lemon juice if needed, and season with salt and pepper.

Store the salsa verde in a glass jar in the fridge for up to a week.

NOTE

I use a mix of fairly equal parts parsley, mint and dill. When it's growing in my garden, I also like to throw in some tarragon.

PORCHETTA

I'm yet to find someone who doesn't get excited at the arrival of a big platter of porchetta at a gathering. Crunchy pork crackling and beautiful, falling-apart tender pork baked with a paste of garlic and lots of fresh herbs – this is such a great option when feeding a crowd. It's also a nod to our honeymoon some 15 years ago, when we visited Tuscany (in January) and had some memorable meals in the streets of Florence, standing around in the freezing cold eating rolls stuffed with hot porchetta and salsa verde, washed down with plastic cups of red wine. So good.

SERVES 8–10
PREP TIME : 20 MINS, PLUS OVERNIGHT 'DRYING'
COOK TIME : 3½ HOURS

2.5–3 kg (5 lb 8 oz–6 lb 12 oz) boned pork
  shoulder, rind scored by your butcher
⅓ cup (40 g) sea salt flakes
2 handfuls mixed herbs (I use sage, parsley,
  marjoram and a little rosemary)

2 Tbsp fennel seeds
1 Tbsp black peppercorns
6 garlic cloves, peeled
2 Tbsp olive oil
1 cup (250 ml) white wine

Fill the kettle and bring it to the boil. Place the pork in your clean sink and pour the boiling water over the top. Pat dry, then rub the salt all over the meat, especially on the scored rind. Place the pork on a rack over a plate and put it in the fridge, uncovered, to 'dry' overnight. (This process makes for extra good crackling so is well worth it, though not essential.)

The next day, remove the pork from the fridge and let it come to room temperature.

Preheat the oven to 120°C (235°F).

Combine the herbs, fennel seeds, peppercorns and garlic on a chopping board and chop, chop, chop until you have a rough, herby paste. (You could do this in a food processor if you prefer.)

Place the pork in a large roasting tin and rub it with the herb paste. Drizzle the olive oil over the top and tie the meat a couple of times down the middle with kitchen string so that it's a neat little parcel. Pop the pork into the oven for 3 hours or until just cooked through. Bump up the heat to as high as it goes – for me that's 250°C (500°F). Pour the wine over the pork and cook for a further 30 minutes to crisp up the crackling.

Remove the pork from the oven and scrape and pour all the pan juices into a little jug. Let the meat rest for at least 30 minutes.

Peel the crackling away from the pork and cut it into smaller pieces, then carve the pork into thick slices. Reheat the pan juices, skimming off some fat if you like, and serve them with the pork, Salsa verde (page 15) and some bread rolls.

More ways to serve this very tasty apricot purée

- Spoon a little into the bottom of a champagne flute and top up with sparkling wine.
- Mix with natural yoghurt and freeze in ice-cream moulds.
- Pour over a pavlova dressed with whipped cream.
- Fold through softened vanilla ice cream, then refreeze for the best apricot ripple ever.
- Whizz it up into a milkshake.
- Serve in a jug alongside a classic baked cheesecake.
- Use as you would a lemon curd to fill meringue cakes or sponges... or anything, really!
- Pour into cute jars, package up and give away to lucky friends, maybe with a bottle of bubbles so they can run with idea number one!

APRICOT MOUSSE

When you're feeding a crowd, the absolute last thing anyone wants is to be dragged into the kitchen to plate up dessert just when things are getting fun. Hence my suggestion is to make up a batch of this beautiful mousse and divide it into cute jars with lids so that all you need to do when it comes to serving is remove them from the fridge, take off the lids and decorate them. I love this recipe so much; it's a light and delicious way to end the meal, as well as the perfect way to showcase the first stone fruit of the season (and my favourite), the apricot. That said, you could swap the apricots with berries, peaches or any other fruit purée.

Apricots and vanilla are my favourite flavour combination of all time. When they come together in this intensely flavoured roasted purée, it's just heaven. The purée is the base for the mousse recipe, but it's also super useful in its own right – see left for some ideas.

SERVES 8–10
PREP TIME : 30 MINS, PLUS SETTING ❳ COOK TIME : 35 MINS

½ cup (125 ml) golden rum
6 gold-strength gelatine leaves (see Note)
⅓ cup (75 g) caster (superfine) sugar,
   or to taste
3 cups (750 ml) single (pure) cream
Persian fairy floss, to serve (optional)

Roasted apricot purée
1.5 kg (3 lb 5 oz) apricots, halved,
   stones removed
½ cup (110 g) caster (superfine) sugar
1 vanilla bean, split lengthways

For the roasted apricot purée, preheat the oven to 180°C (350°F) and place the fruit in an ovenproof dish or roasting tin. Sprinkle the sugar over the top. Scrape the vanilla seeds into the dish and add the scraped pod. Pour in ¼ cup (60 ml) water and bake for about 30 minutes or until the apricots are completely softened.

Discard the vanilla bean. Blitz the apricots in a blender or food processor to make a smooth purée. Pour the purée into a clean jar and pop it into the fridge to cool completely.

Pour the rum into a small saucepan and bring just to boiling point. Remove from the heat, add the gelatine leaves and give a little stir to help them dissolve.

Put 3 cups (750 ml) of the apricot purée in a bowl, add the rum mixture and stir to combine. Check for sweetness – add the sugar if you think it's necessary. Place the bowl in the freezer for 30 minutes, then give the mixture a good stir and return it to the freezer for 1 hour.

Whip the cream until soft peaks form, then gently fold it into the chilled apricot mixture. Divide the mousse among jars for serving (or just transfer it to one large serving dish), cover and pop it into the fridge to set for at least 3 hours.

Just before serving, dollop a spoonful of the apricot purée on top of each mousse and pile a little cloud of Persian fairy floss on top, if using.

NOTE
If you're using powdered gelatine, use a ratio of 7 g (⅛ oz) to set 2 cups (500 ml) liquid for a mousse-like consistency.

All at sea

I've lived on our farm among gum trees, hills, scrub, sometimes dust and sometimes tall green grass for 15 years and hopefully many more to come. But my childhood was spent by the sea and, almost daily, swimming in it. Any visits to family and friends on the coast are precious, especially days like this one.

My school friend Poppy, her husband Rupert and their boys Oliver, Henry, Tom and Eddie live on Sydney's northern beaches, where they also run Beachwood Designs together. As often as they can, they spend a day or a weekend out on their beautifully restored wooden boat Olah (for lovers of wooden boats, it's a pretty special old Halvorsen). This time, we joined them. I provided lunch, they brought the boat, and it was just one of those happy, shiny pennies of a day that gets put straight into the special memories box.

Driving home afterwards, I wondered, why don't we do this more often? It's really not that hard to get away, to call up friends and say: you bring this thing (in this case, a boat!), we'll bring that thing and then, after nine or so hours of driving and far less time than that in the kitchen, it all comes together. And at the end of it all, you have a day to remember.

This menu is not at all difficult, it's not expensive and all ages seem to love it. And, like all food, it tastes best in good company.

Poppy's ideas for entertaining on a boat

We try to get out on the boat as a family every Sunday. I always have linen tea towels, old-style cutlery, cheese knives, timber cutting boards, ceramic plates and champagne on hand, keeping with the style and feel of the Halvorsen. I rely on these things, and the cushions and throws, to enhance the flavour of the food! I usually bring plenty of cheeses, dips and crackers or carrots to keep the kids going while they explore, row, paddle, fish and swim. Typically we'll do lunch on the barbecue (often pork sausages) with fresh bread bought on the way, tomatoes, avocados, mayonnaise and chutney. Friends coming onboard usually bring a cake and cream for afterwards, or we simply have some form of chocolate.

@beachwooddesigns

ASPARAGUS *with* ADOBO CHILLI BUTTER
Jewelled RICE PILAF
BARBECUED LAMB SHOULDER *with*
whipped feta and pistachio crumbs
ORANGE AND HONEY *melt-and-mix* CAKE

It was one of those happy, shiny pennies of a day that gets put straight into the special memories box.

ASPARAGUS *with* ADOBO CHILLI BUTTER

This recipe makes much more of the chilli butter than you need, but it's so completely delicious that you'll want a stash in the fridge for flavour emergencies. It's excellent alongside a barbecued steak, in a baked potato, rubbed under the skin of a chook before roasting or tossed through a lemony rice pilaf. Here, when dotted on top of a platter of beautiful blanched asparagus, it makes a lovely spring side dish.

SERVES 6-8 (MAKES ABOUT 1 CUP CHILLI BUTTER)
PREP TIME: 10 MINS ⅝ COOK TIME: 5 MINS

20 asparagus spears, woody ends snapped off

Adobo chilli butter
1 small bunch coriander (cilantro)
Grated zest and juice of 1 lime
4 Tbsp chipotle chillies in adobo sauce,
    finely chopped
1 cup (250 g) unsalted butter, softened

For the adobo chilli butter, finely chop the coriander stalks and leaves and pop them in a bowl. Add the lime zest and juice, chillies and butter and mix well. Season to taste with sea salt and freshly ground black pepper.

Bring a large saucepan of salted water to the boil. Plunge the asparagus into the boiling water and cook for 1 minute, then drain and transfer to a platter. Top with 3 tablespoons of the chilli butter and gently toss with the asparagus so it melts into a delicious, flavourful puddle.

Jewelled RICE PILAF

Hands down, this is my favourite way to cook rice. Full of flavour, colour, crunch and gorgeous-looking, this pilaf is great as a bed for the barbecued lamb shoulder, but is also fabulous as a side dish for all kinds of barbecued or roasted meats. I would also happily serve it on its own, perhaps with a bowl of greens and a few boiled eggs on the side for protein. Either way, it's lovely hot or at room temperature, which makes it ideal for picnics.

SERVES 6-8
PREP TIME: 20 MINS ⅝ COOK TIME: 45 MINS

1/4 cup (60 ml) olive oil
3 brown onions, thinly sliced
2 cups (400 g) basmati rice
1/2 tsp ground cumin
1/2 tsp ground coriander
1 cinnamon stick
700 ml (24 fl oz) chicken or vegetable stock
Grated zest of 1 orange
3/4 cup (95 g) slivered almonds
3/4 cup (110 g) dried apricots, roughly chopped
    and soaked in cold water for 10 mins
1 bunch chives, finely chopped
Seeds of 1 pomegranate

Heat the olive oil in a large, deep frying pan with a lid over medium heat (I've used a lid of foil and it was fine). Cook the onion for 15–20 minutes or until soft and caramelised. Add the rice and spices and cook, stirring, for another 5 minutes. Stir in the stock and grated orange zest. Cover the pan, reduce the heat to as low as possible and cook the rice for 20 minutes.

Meanwhile, toast the almonds in a dry frying pan until golden.

Once the rice is fluffy and tender, remove the pan from the heat. Stir in the almonds and the drained apricot pieces.

Just before serving, stir the chives through the pilaf and sprinkle the pomegranate seeds over the top.

BARBECUED LAMB SHOULDER
with whipped feta and pistachio crumbs

Lamb shoulder usually finds itself being slow roasted, but here it is seasoned and barbecued to become the beautifully tender star of this lunch. The bonus of using shoulder is that it's much more economical than the more traditional backstrap or other barbecuing cuts.

Here I've served the sliced lamb on top of the Jewelled rice pilaf (page 22), sprinkled with the pistachio crumbs, and added a bowl of whipped feta and a stack of soft wraps. I find kids especially like to make their lunch this way, spreading the wrap with the feta and topping it with the lamb, pilaf and a few asparagus spears. The whipped feta does make a large quantity, but it's so yummy that I'm always happy to have leftovers in the fridge.

SERVES 6-8
PREP TIME: 30 MINS, PLUS 30 MINS MARINATING ❧ COOK TIME: 55 MINS

2 kg (4 lb 8 oz) boneless lamb shoulder
12 anchovies
1/4 cup (60 ml) olive oil

Pistachio crumbs
4 large slices sourdough bread
1 cup (150 g) pistachios
1 handful mint leaves, finely chopped
1 handful parsley leaves, finely chopped
Grated zest of 1 lemon

Whipped feta
300 g (10 1/2 oz) smooth feta cheese,
    at room temperature
300 g (10 1/2 oz) cream cheese, softened
1/3 cup (80 ml) olive oil
Grated zest and juice of 1 lemon

Prepare the pistachio crumbs. Preheat the oven to 180°C (350°F). Tear the sourdough into pieces and blitz in a food processor until it forms coarse breadcrumbs. Spread the crumbs over a baking tray and bake for 15 minutes or until golden brown, tossing halfway through so the crumbs cook evenly. Tip the crumbs into a large bowl. Spread the pistachios on the tray and bake for 10 minutes or until they are just beginning to turn golden. Roughly chop the pistachios, then add them to the bowl with the breadcrumbs. Add the mint, parsley and lemon zest and season with a little sea salt.

Put the lamb shoulder on a chopping board and press down to flatten it. Cut the lamb into three or four pieces. Mix the anchovies and olive oil with some salt and pepper and rub the mixture over the lamb. Leave to marinate at room temperature for 30 minutes.

Meanwhile, put all the ingredients for the whipped feta in the clean food processor bowl and whizz until combined. Transfer the mixture to a bowl and give it a good stir with a wooden spoon to lighten the consistency. Season to taste. (Serve this at room temperature so it keeps its lovely light consistency – a little time in the fridge will firm it up quite a lot.)

Heat a barbecue grill to medium–high. Cook the lamb pieces on the hottest part of the grill for 15 minutes on each side. Rest the lamb for 10 minutes before slicing across the grain.

Spread the whipped feta over the base of a large platter, arrange the sliced lamb on top and sprinkle with the pistachio crumbs.

ORANGE AND HONEY *melt-and-mix* CAKE

This delicately flavoured honey cake is one of those wonderful recipes that you really can get into the oven within 10 minutes of deciding to make it. I also love that it smells and tastes a little bit like gingerbread, but is still fluffy and light. These quantities make one large slab cake, but you could halve them to make a 20 cm (8 inch) cake.

SERVES 6–8 (WITH LEFTOVERS)
PREP TIME: 10 MINS 〉 COOK TIME: 50 MINS

150 g (5¹/2 oz) butter
1³/4 cups (260 g) self-raising flour
1/2 cup (100 g) dark brown sugar
2/3 cup (235 g) honey
1 tsp ground cinnamon
1/2 tsp ground ginger
1/4 tsp freshly grated nutmeg
3 eggs
3/4 cup (200 g) natural yoghurt
3 blood oranges, peeled and cut into small pieces

Icing
1 cup (125 g) icing (confectioners') sugar
Grated zest and juice of 1 lemon

Preheat the oven to 180°C (350°F). Grease a deep 30 x 20 cm (12 x 8 inch) roasting tin and line the tin with baking paper.

Melt the butter and set aside to cool for at least 5 minutes.

Combine the flour, brown sugar, honey, spices, eggs, yoghurt and cooled butter in a food processor. Whizz for 1 minute or until you have a smooth batter.

Pour the batter into the lined tin, smooth the top and dot with the orange pieces. Bake for 45 minutes or until a skewer inserted in the middle of the cake comes out clean. Leave the cake to cool for 10 minutes before lifting it out of the tin and transferring it to a wire rack to cool completely.

For the icing, whisk together the icing sugar, lemon zest and juice until thick and smooth. Pour the icing over the cake and serve it in lovely big wedges.

You really can get this cake into the oven within 10 minutes of deciding to make it!

Spring chicken lunch party

My mum and dad's farm plays a big role in our family life. For just over 30 years it has been the place where we come to be together, and the house they have built here holds many memories for my siblings and me, and these days, for our children, too.

This is where Tim and I had our wedding reception. It's where we do Christmas, school holiday art camps with the cousins (Mum is an artist and wonderful teacher) and weekends when we can, with as many as we can. It was pretty special for me to capture one such time catching up with my brother, parents, cousins, husband, kids and niece for a sunny spring lunch under the crabapple tree by the kitchen.

Anyone who knows me knows I love a tray bake – a dish that requires only a little simple assemblage before popping into the oven to take care of itself while you have a nice time in good company. This meal is exactly that: a very easy dish of chicken swimming in super-tasty juices (hence the bread for mopping) that feels just smart enough for company but also friendly enough for everyone to feel relaxed and excited about while they get on with the conversation and catch ups.

Whether the family you love sharing meals with is the one you were born with or the friends who have become family, or both, I hope you enjoy cooking this menu together, with the ones you love.

HERB BOUQUET *with sunflower seed pesto* ❯ Mini POMMES ANNA
Julie Delpy-style CHICKEN WITH CALVADOS *and crème fraîche*
Crusty bread ❯ *Blanched asparagus with* BEARNAISE SAUCE *(page 79)*
CHOCOLATE, HAZELNUT *and* ESPRESSO CAKE

*Family meals require tasty, easy, crowd-pleasing dishes
that look after themselves in the oven while you
get on with the catching up.*

HERB BOUQUET
with sunflower seed pesto

About ten years ago I was lucky enough to visit Copenhagen on a press trip. A small bunch of food writers from around the world were brought together to sample some of the city's best food and markets, and it was a dream! We were treated to some extraordinary dishes and food experiences, but the one that left the biggest impression was a tiny, beautiful posy of herbs held together with a nut paste and tied with a celery ribbon at Restaurant Relae.

I loved the idea of starting a meal with something so fresh, pretty and delicious, and try to do a similar version at home when the herbs in our garden are varied enough. It's really lovely to place a herb bouquet on each plate setting and then enjoy it as a starter, along with some warm bread and nice butter or olive oil.

SERVES 6–8 AS A STARTER
PREP TIME : 20 MINS ⟩ COOK TIME : 1 MIN

3 long celery stalks
1 baby cos lettuce, leaves separated
1 handful sorrel, chervil, tarragon, mint, parsley and/or basil
1 handful edible flowers (optional)

Sunflower seed pesto
1/3 cup (50 g) pine nuts
1/3 cup (55 g) sunflower seeds
1/3 cup (35 g) finely grated parmesan cheese
A squeeze of lemon juice
A pinch of salt
1/4 cup (60 ml) extra virgin olive oil

First make the pesto. Toast the nuts and seeds in a dry frying pan until golden, then tip into a food processor or blender. Add the parmesan, lemon juice, salt and olive oil and blitz until you have a rough paste (you want a bit of texture to offset the beautiful soft herbs).

Cut two of the celery stalks into 10 cm (4 inch) batons, about 5 mm (1/4 inch) thick. Take the remaining celery stalk and, holding it in the middle, use a vegetable peeler to grate long thin strips. Blanch the celery batons and strips in salted boiling water for 20 seconds, then plunge into a bowl of cold water. Place the bowl in the fridge until needed.

To assemble, brush six (or eight, if you're serving eight people) of the bigger lettuce leaves with the pesto and top each with a smaller lettuce leaf. Add the herbs from largest to smallest, using a little pesto to stick the leaves together. Place a celery baton in the middle, then gently tie the base together with the celery ribbons. Pop the edible flowers in the middle of the tie, if using, and keep chilled until you are ready to sit down. (Please note that these gorgeous little posies will start to wilt after an hour or so in the fridge.)

Mini POMMES ANNA

Elegant, delicious, easy and another make-ahead winner, these little potato stacks are dinner-party gold. I find they hold together better if they're chilled before you turn them out of the muffin tin, but if you don't have time for that it's not the end of the world. They might not be as uniform, but they'll still taste fabulous.

SERVES 6–8
PREP TIME : 20 MINS, PLUS CHILLING ⟩ COOK TIME : 1 HOUR

½ cup (125 g) butter
3 Tbsp thyme leaves
2 garlic cloves, finely chopped
2 tsp sea salt
6–8 waxy potatoes

Preheat the oven to 200°C (400°F). Melt the butter in a small saucepan. Brush each cavity of a 12-hole, 1 cup (250 ml) muffin tin with a little of the melted butter. Stir the thyme, garlic and salt into the remaining melted butter.

Peel and very thinly slice the potatoes (I use a mandolin for this). Place in a bowl, add the melted butter mixture and gently toss to combine.

Stack the potato slices in the muffin holes, pressing down as you go. Cover with foil and bake for about 40 minutes or until the potatoes are completely cooked through. Remove from the oven and set aside to cool. At this stage, pop the tin into the fridge for a few hours or overnight.

Preheat the oven to 200°C (400°F). Line a baking tray with baking paper. Gently invert the potato cakes onto the tray and bake for 25–30 minutes or until crispy and golden.

These little potato stacks are dinner-party gold.

Recipes pictured page 34

Julie Delpy-style CHICKEN WITH CALVADOS *and crème fraîche*

This dish is a belated ode to a girl I met at university in Canberra many years ago. She was French and beautiful, and looked a bit like Julie Delpy, and she could actually cook and host grown-up dinner parties. This was something that made quite the impression on me, having come straight from boarding school to residential college and being yet to venture into a kitchen of my own.

One night, a small group of us escaped the horrible pizza and soggy chips of our college kitchen for dinner at her parents' place. She cooked chicken with calvados and cream and we even drank wine out of a bottle, not a cask. It was one of the best meals of my twenties. And here's my take on it. It's absolutely delicious and easy to throw together, and it has become a firm family favourite.

SERVES 6–8
PREP TIME : 15 MINS 〉 COOK TIME : 55 MINS

8 chicken thigh cutlets, skin on (see Notes)
1/3 cup (90 g) wholegrain mustard
1/3 cup (85 g) crème fraîche (or sour cream at a pinch)
3 garlic cloves, finely chopped
Grated zest of 1 lemon
1/3 cup (80 ml) olive oil
1 small handful thyme sprigs
1/4 cup (60 ml) calvados (see Notes)

Preheat the oven to 200°C (400°F). Place the chicken in a roasting tin, skin side up. The tin should be large enough for all of the chicken pieces to sit fairly snugly in a single layer.

Whisk the mustard, crème fraîche, garlic, lemon zest and olive oil in a bowl. Rub the mixture over the chicken, add the thyme sprigs to the tin and pour half of the calvados over the top. Bake the chicken for 30 minutes.

Pour in the rest of the calvados and bake for a final 20 minutes. Transfer the chicken to a plate and cover with foil.

Pour all of the pan juices into a small saucepan and whisk over medium–high heat until thickened and slightly reduced, about 5 minutes. Pour the sauce over the chicken and serve with the Mini pommes Anna (page 32).

NOTES

If you can only get skinless chicken thigh cutlets, that's fine; they just won't look as golden as the ones in the picture.

Calvados is a French apple brandy that you won't regret buying, I promise! It's just delicious served neat on the rocks or mixed with a good ginger beer and ice. White wine or vermouth would be a good substitute.

CHOCOLATE, HAZELNUT
and ESPRESSO CAKE

I have been making this cake for many years. It was a staple and popular dessert item when we used to run farm tours and lunches every month and here's why: it's really stable, in the sense that you can make it a day or two ahead, wrap it tightly and it will be even nicer. Plus, the flavour combination of chocolate, hazelnut and coffee is a proven winner, and it's not at all hard to throw together. I've served this with poached pears on the side, with ice cream, with cream and just on its own. It's always beautiful.

This recipe makes quite a large cake but it does last well for a few days and a little slice with coffee makes a lovely morning tea. Plus it freezes well.

SERVES 6–8 (WITH LEFTOVERS)
PREP TIME : 20 MINS ⅜ COOK TIME : 45 MINS

5 eggs
3/4 cup (165 g) firmly packed brown sugar
1 shot (30 ml/1 fl oz) espresso coffee
2 3/4 cups (410 g) chopped dark chocolate
1 cup (250 g) unsalted butter, chopped
100 g (3 1/2 oz) hazelnut meal
1 1/2 tsp baking powder
1 tsp vanilla extract
A pinch of salt
Thick (double) cream, to serve
Fresh raspberries, to serve

Preheat the oven to 150°C (300°F). Grease a 24 cm (9 1/2 inch) spring-form tin. Line the tin with baking paper.

Using an electric mixer, beat the eggs and half the brown sugar for at least 5 minutes or until pale and fluffy and doubled in size.

Combine the remaining brown sugar, coffee, chocolate and butter in a heatproof bowl over a saucepan of simmering water. Cook, stirring often, until you have a smooth, shiny mixture.

Pour the chocolate mixture into the egg and sugar mixture and very gently fold together. Add the hazelnut meal, baking powder, vanilla and salt and gently fold together.

Transfer the batter to the cake tin and smooth the top. Bake for 40 minutes or until the cake feels just set in the middle. Leave to cool for 10 minutes before removing from the tin.

Serve the cake warm or at room temperature, with the cream and raspberries.

Keeping the kids happy

After we had kids, our next few years of entertaining often involved sausage sandwiches for the kids, and getting that first 'dinner service' out of the way before sitting the adults down for a more interesting meal. There's nothing wrong with that, of course – I'm yet to find a child who doesn't love a sausage sandwich! But sometimes it's nice to try a few different, tastier and more vibrant options. And I do believe that when you make a bit of an effort to produce kid-friendly food that looks and tastes really good, even the smallest person at the table will appreciate it (even if they don't come out with those exact words).

On this occasion, a hot February evening, I packed up some favourite kid-friendly dishes, jumped in the car and headed for photographer Clancy Job's place just out of Narromine in western New South Wales. It was a total delight feeding her four sweet, friendly and incredibly gorgeous kids (and one chook). To make the evening extra special, it had rained that afternoon for the first time in a while so we ended dinner with a bit of a paddle in the paddock.

All of these dishes are very 'young person friendly', but with a jar of chilli, some kimchi or other spicier condiments on the table, they'll hit the spot with all ages.

Clancy's tips on feeding a horde of kids

The warmer months are my favourite and I love nothing more than having friends and their kids over for a meal. I always feed them outside (mostly because we have a really small kitchen and things can get out of control quickly with a multitude of kids and greasy barbecued sausages!). I find that when there is a bunch of kids, they are too busy playing to sit and eat a proper meal, so a big 'picking' platter works well. They can grab some tucker and run off and continue to play bullrush, then return for another handful. I serve food on a trestle table on the lawn, or make up a little picnic on our jacaranda deck. Kids gravitate to this area as we have swings hanging from the jacaranda tree, plus it's a great height for little people.

@clancyjob

Kid-style SOBORO DON ⸙ *Crunchy, tangy* CUCUMBER SALAD
ZINGY CARROT *and ginger* SALAD
WARM FRUIT SALAD *with malt crumbs*

When you make an effort to produce kid-friendly food that looks and tastes really good, even the smallest person at the table will appreciate it.

Kid-style SOBORO DON

This is a really simple recipe that everyone always loves. I serve it poke-bowl style so that everyone can make up their own, which kids particularly love, with the chicken, cucumber salad (page 42), carrot salad (page 42), sushi rice, omelette strips and spring onions in separate bowls.

SERVES 4–6 KIDS
PREP TIME : 10 MINS ❧ COOK TIME : 10 MINS

1 Tbsp brown sugar
¼ cup (60 ml) soy sauce
¼ cup (60 ml) mirin
4 cm (1½ inch) piece ginger, peeled and finely grated
2 Tbsp vegetable oil
500 g (1 lb 2 oz) chicken mince
2 cups (420 g) sushi rice, cooked according to the packet instructions
1 large handful snow peas (mange tout), trimmed
2 spring onions (scallions), cut into strips

Omelette strips
4 eggs
1 Tbsp vegetable oil
2 spring onions (scallions), finely chopped

Combine the brown sugar, soy sauce, mirin and ginger in a jar and shake well.

Heat the oil in a large heavy-based saucepan over high heat. Cook the chicken, stirring to break up any lumps, for a few minutes or until almost cooked through. Add the soy sauce mixture and cook for another minute or so.

For the omelette strips, whisk the eggs together until well combined. Heat the oil in a large frying pan over medium–high heat, pour in the egg and cook for a couple of minutes. Add the spring onion, gently flip one half of the omelette over the other and cook for 1 minute. Slide the omelette onto a plate and cut it into strips.

Serve the chicken and omelette strips in bowls with the sushi rice, snow peas and spring onion strips.

Variation

Pour the soy sauce mixture over 500 g (1 lb 2 oz) salmon cubes. Marinate for an hour or so, then transfer the salmon to a foil-lined tray and cook under a hot grill for 7 minutes or until just cooked through and beginning to caramelise. My kids call this 'pink fish' and it has long been a favourite.

Crunchy, tangy
CUCUMBER SALAD

This salad is verging very close to pickle territory, which is probably why I love it so much. It brings pep and colour to loads of simple dishes (even a simple fried egg and brown rice feels fancy with this piled on top) and, when sprinkled with a little chilli, it's one of my favourite things.

SERVES 4

PREP TIME : 10 MINS } COOK TIME : NIL

4 Lebanese (short) cucumbers, halved and
   thinly sliced
1/2 red onion, thinly sliced
3 spring onions (scallions), sliced
1 bunch coriander (cilantro), leaves picked
1 scant handful mint leaves
1–2 red chillies, finely chopped (optional)

Dressing
1/3 cup (80 ml) rice wine vinegar
1 Tbsp sesame oil
Juice of 2 lemons
1 Tbsp brown sugar
1 tsp sea salt

Combine the cucumber, red onion, spring onion, coriander and mint leaves in a bowl.

Whisk the dressing ingredients together, then pour the mixture over the salad and gently toss together to combine. Cover and place in the fridge until needed.

Serve the cucumber salad with the red chilli on the side, if using.

ZINGY CARROT
and ginger SALAD

Bright, crunchy and tasty, this salad is one of my big favourites. And most kids love it, too (though you can't win them all!). Double the recipe and keep some for your lunch the next day – I love it on a bed of yoghurt with some nigella seeds, a dollop of harissa and a boiled egg.

SERVES 4-6

PREP TIME : 10 MINS } COOK TIME : NIL

400 g (14 oz) carrots, cut into matchsticks
   or grated
1/2 cup (70 g) unsalted peanuts, toasted and
   roughly chopped

Dressing
Juice of 2 limes
1 Tbsp sesame oil
4 cm (1 1/2 inch) piece ginger, peeled and
   finely grated

Combine the dressing ingredients in a jar and shake to combine.

Place the carrots and peanuts in a serving bowl and toss with the dressing.

NOTE

If making this ahead, keep the carrot matchsticks in a bowl of cold water in the fridge to stop them from discolouring. (This is also a good way to store cut-up carrots as they stay crunchier.) When you're ready to assemble the salad, drain the carrots and toss them with the remaining ingredients.

More ideas for keeping the kids happy

- Prepare the salmon variation of the soboro don and toss it with some cooked soba noodles and the cucumber salad. You could also use poached chicken or hot-smoked trout.

- Make up a batch of simple fried rice and top it with the carrot salad for the kids. Stir through some kimchi for those who like it a bit spicier. Top each serving with a fried egg, sliced spring onions (scallions) and edamame beans.

- Make a double batch of the soboro don and roll the left-over chicken and rice into balls about the size of a golf ball. Shallow-fry or bake until heated through, pouring the soy sauce dressing over the balls once they're reheated. Serve with green miso.

- Open a big tin of tuna and serve it with the cucumber salad, carrot salad and a few big lettuce leaves to scoop everything up.

WARM FRUIT SALAD
with malt crumbs

This is basically my son Tom's idea of heaven – a big platter of sweet, warm berries with melted chocolate and malt crumbs. I love this dessert as it's super easy to make (the malt crumbs can be made well in advance and stored in a jar) and it's a great way to make use of your favourite seasonal fruit. This is also beautiful made with apricots and raspberries during summertime.

SERVES 6
PREP TIME : 15 MINS ⟩ COOK TIME : 40 MINS

600 g (1 lb 5 oz) mixed berries (strawberries and blackberries are good)
1/3 cup (75 g) caster (superfine) sugar
Juice of 1 orange
1/2 cup (85 g) milk chocolate chips
Vanilla ice cream, to serve

Malt crumbs
1 cup (120 g) malted milk powder
1/2 cup (75 g) plain (all-purpose) flour
1/2 cup (110 g) caster (superfine) sugar
140 g (5 oz) chilled unsalted butter, cut into cubes

To make the malt crumbs, preheat the oven to 180°C (350°F). Line a baking tray with baking paper. Combine the malted milk powder, flour and sugar in a bowl and rub in the butter to form a crumble-like mixture. (You can also do this step in a food processor.) Spread the crumb mixture over the tray and bake for about 20 minutes or until pale golden. Cool completely on the tray, then store in an airtight container.

Preheat the oven to 160°C (320°F). Place the berries in a large roasting tin and sprinkle with the sugar. Squeeze the orange juice over the berries and sprinkle with the chocolate chips. Roast for 20 minutes or until the berries are soft and collapsed, and the chocolate has melted.

Scatter the malt crumbs over the warm fruit salad and serve with vanilla ice cream.

Spring supper picnic

Spring serves up its fair share of chilly afternoons, but after a long winter cooped up by the fire, we're all busting to get outside. Why not rug up, pack up some goodies and extend the weekend with an early dinner picnic?

Sunday afternoons for the Walmsley family of Buena Vista Farm are a moment to pause and take a breath after a weekend of farm tours, workshops, milking and feeding goats on this beautiful and highly productive coastal farm. It was such a pleasure to share a picnic with them on a chilly spring Sunday in the tall grass of their front paddock, which also happens to overlook a pretty spectacular piece of the coast in Gerringong. Aside from the odd errant goat investigating our picnic basket (I'm looking at you, Daphne!), it was the perfect end to a busy weekend.

Fiona's take on sharing her love of food and hosting

Adam and I have always loved hosting. Many years ago we began hosting long degustations with matching wines for our friends, with the occasional medieval feast thrown in for fun! I love cooking, and Adam loves people, and we love entertaining together. These days our gatherings usually involve a bit less preparation and many more small people, and we love them just as much. We reckon the secret is planning and a good list. You can throw together the most complicated thing if you have a good prep list and everything on hand. You don't want to be rushing around at the last minute – no-one wants a flustered host! We keep sparkling wine on hand, as well as goat's cheese and crackers, so if people unexpectedly show up there's always goat's cheese and fun, with no effort.

@buenavistafarm

Fiona's OLIVE OIL CRACKERS *with cheese and pickles*
Easy TOMATO *and* CHORIZO STEW *with sourdough*
GINGER CRUNCH BARS *with custard and rhubarb*

Why not rug up, pack up some goodies and
extend the weekend with an early dinner picnic?

Fiona's OLIVE OIL CRACKERS

Fiona serves these crackers with her goat's cheese and pickles, both as a family snack and also to farm guests. Ever since she sent me the recipe, I've been doing the same. These are so, so easy and quick to make, and flaky and delicious – this recipe is definitely one to bookmark! I've made them with rosemary but also swapped it for fennel and chilli, which was delicious. Lemon thyme leaves would also be great.

MAKES ABOUT 40
PREP TIME : 15 MINS } COOK TIME : 10 MINS

2 cups (300 g) plain (all-purpose) flour
3/4 cup (185 ml) olive oil
1 Tbsp finely chopped rosemary
2 tsp sea salt flakes

Preheat the oven to 180°C (350°F). Line two baking trays with baking paper.

Put the flour, olive oil, rosemary, sea salt and 1/2 cup (125 ml) water in a bowl and mix until well combined.

Divide the dough into two balls. Roll out one ball of dough between two sheets of baking paper until it's as thin as you can make it (or use a pasta maker if you have one). Cut the dough into squares or strips with a knife (I used a ridged ravioli cutter for those pretty edges) and place them on the trays. Repeat with the remaining dough.

Bake the crackers for 10 minutes or until crisp and pale golden. Allow them to cool completely on a wire rack and then transfer to an airtight container.

These are so, so easy and quick to make, and flaky and delicious.

Easy TOMATO *and* CHORIZO STEW

This warming, flavour-punch of a tomato stew is a pretty wonderful thing to pour into a big mug and wrap your fingers around on a windswept headland on a cool spring evening. Not all of us have our own headland for such occasions, but you probably have a garden, nature strip, nearby park or beach. Pack this stew in a thermos for your dinner picnic and serve it with some warm sourdough or the garlic bread from page 137. We crumbled a little of Fiona and Adam's fresh goat's cheese over the stew and it added such a lovely note of creamy, tangy goodness – highly recommended!

SERVES 6
PREP TIME : 15 MINS ⟩ COOK TIME : 50 MINUTES

1 Tbsp olive oil
1 tsp fennel seeds
2 chorizo sausages, diced
3 garlic cloves, sliced
2 brown onions, diced
1 carrot, finely diced
1 celery stalk, finely diced
1 cup (250 ml) white wine
800 g (1 lb 12 oz) tin whole peeled tomatoes
250 g (9 oz) soft goat's cheese, to serve

Heat the olive oil in a large saucepan over medium–high heat. Add the fennel seeds and cook for 1 minute or until aromatic. Add the chorizo and cook for a few more minutes, then add the garlic, onion, carrot and celery. Cook, stirring often, for 10 minutes.

Pour in the wine and cook for 1 minute or until the liquid bubbles and reduces a little. Add the tomatoes and cook, breaking everything up with a spoon. Reduce the heat, season with salt and freshly ground black pepper and gently simmer for about 30 minutes, stirring every now and then so the stew doesn't catch and burn on the base of the pan.

Either serve the stew straight away, or transfer it to a thermos to keep hot and head off to your picnic. Crumble the goat's cheese over the stew and serve it with some lovely warm sourdough or garlic bread.

Variation

You could use this stew as a base for a quick and easy seafood stew. Bring the stew to the boil, then reduce the heat to low and add 800 g (1 lb 12 oz) mixed seafood (e.g. mussels, firm white fish, calamari). Cook for about 5 minutes or until the fish is cooked through and the mussel shells have opened.

Recipe pictured page 51

GINGER CRUNCH BARS
with custard and rhubarb

The idea of dipping crunchy ginger bars into cups of warm custard and rhubarb compote while sitting on a windswept beach, all rugged up with friends, screams Enid Blyton-style adventures, don't you think? Ginger, custard and rhubarb are one of my all-time favourite flavour combinations and come together here in a delicious, portable and easy pudding.

The ginger bars are a really lovely, crunchy biscuit. They're very quick to make and they store well, so perhaps prepare a double batch and pop some into bags for a sweet little gift for your ginger-loving friends. I also love them crumbled over or stirred through ice cream.

SERVES 6
PREP TIME : 15 MINS ❱ COOK TIME : 30 MINS

150 g (5$^{1}/_{2}$ oz) butter
$^{1}/_{2}$ cup (110 g) caster (superfine) sugar
$^{1}/_{4}$ cup (90 g) golden syrup
2 cups (190 g) rolled oats
$^{1}/_{2}$ cup (75 g) plain (all-purpose) flour
$^{1}/_{2}$ cup (45 g) desiccated coconut
$^{1}/_{2}$ tsp baking powder
2 tsp ground ginger
$^{1}/_{2}$ tsp ground cinnamon
Sophia's rhubarb compote (page 138)

Thick vanilla custard
2 cups (500 ml) full-cream milk
1 vanilla bean, split lengthways
4 egg yolks
$^{1}/_{4}$ cup (55 g) caster (superfine) sugar
2 Tbsp cornflour (cornstarch)

Preheat the oven to 170°C (340°F). Grease and line a 20 cm (8 inch) square cake tin.

Stir the butter, sugar and golden syrup in a small saucepan over medium heat until melted.

Combine the oats, flour, coconut, baking powder and spices in a food processor and give a quick pulse so the oats are broken up and the mixture resembles wholemeal flour. Tip the oat mixture into a bowl and stir in the butter mixture.

Press the mixture evenly into the tin and bake for 15 minutes or until golden. Leave in the tin to cool for a few minutes and then cut into bars. Cool completely, then pack into a large jar.

To make the custard, pour the milk into a saucepan. Scrape the vanilla seeds into the pan and add the scraped pod. Cook over medium–high heat until the milk reaches boiling point.

Meanwhile, whisk the egg yolks, sugar and cornflour in a heatproof bowl until pale and fluffy. Strain a little of the hot milk into the egg mixture and whisk to combine, then pour in the rest of the milk, whisking as you go so the eggs don't cook and curdle. Return the mixture to the saucepan and stir over low heat for about 6 minutes or until the mixture thickens and coats the back of a spoon. Pour the custard into a thermos to keep warm for your picnic or pour it into a bottle, seal and place in the fridge until needed.

To serve, pour the custard into cups or bowls, then top it with a spoonful of the rhubarb compote. Use the ginger bars to dip and swirl the custard and rhubarb together and scoop it up in delicious, comforting mouthfuls.

Working lunch

Not too long ago, if you moved to the country you also had to change careers – remote working just wasn't a thing like it is now. And while farming is an incredible career, it doesn't suit everyone's skills or passions. But these days, we can pretty much do any job anywhere. We can work remotely, run creative businesses from kitchen tables 10 hours west of Sydney, connect and create communities despite (and sometimes because of) the tyranny of distance.

Like hundreds of other rural women, I work from home and share the farm office with my husband (and often the kids). And while I do love the flexibility of working from home, I also miss the buzzy environment of my Sydney working days on the editorial team of a national food magazine. So these days, as often as possible, I use one of the many co-working spaces that are popping up in towns like mine and in Dubbo, home to the venue for this get-together. The Exchange is a co-working space and community hub for freelancers, entrepreneurs and remotely working employees.

All of these recipes are easy to make and will keep for a few days in the fridge. Go nuts on a Sunday afternoon, pack your salads into a few different containers and then you can just grab and go, and get on with building your empire.

GREEK SALAD *with* CHICKEN, RISONI *and caramelised lemon*
RED CABBAGE *and* QUINOA SALAD *with candied walnuts*
RAINBOW PICKLE *and* GRUYERE TOASTIES
CACAO, BANANA *and* PEANUT BUTTER SMOOTHIE

All of these recipes are easy to make and will keep for a few days in the fridge.

GREEK SALAD *with* CHICKEN, RISONI *and caramelised lemon*

This is just gorgeous and could easily stand up to being a main course for dinner or a lunch party on its own – just add a green salad and some toasted flatbread or similar. You could also leave out the chicken and make it a vegetarian salad, or serve it as a side dish to barbecued meats.

SERVES 6
PREP TIME : 20 MINS ╳ COOK TIME : 45 MINS

1 cup (220 g) risoni pasta
1/3 cup (80 ml) olive oil
2 lemons, thickly sliced
2 red capsicums (peppers), halved and seeded
200 g (7 oz) feta cheese
1/2 red onion, thinly sliced
250 g (9 oz) mixed cherry tomatoes, halved or quartered if large
1 large telegraph cucumber, cut into chunks
400 g (14 oz) shredded roast chicken (or purchased barbecued chicken)
2 Tbsp nigella seeds

Cook the risoni according to the packet instructions, then drain and leave to cool while you prepare the rest of your salad.

Heat half of the olive oil in a large heavy-based frying pan over medium–high heat. Add the lemon slices and cook for 5 minutes on each side or until soft and caramelised. Remove from the pan and set aside to cool.

Return the pan to the heat and cook the capsicum halves for 5 minutes or so on each side. Reduce the heat, cover and cook for another 15 minutes or until the capsicum halves are very soft and cooked through. Cool slightly, then roughly chop.

Meanwhile, break the feta into chunks and place in a bowl with the remaining olive oil, the lemon slices and red onion. Mix to combine and season to taste.

Gently fold the risoni through the feta and lemon mixture. Add the cherry tomatoes, cucumber, capsicum and chicken and fold together. Store the salad in the fridge but bring it to room temperature before serving, sprinkled with the nigella seeds.

RED CABBAGE *and* QUINOA SALAD
with candied walnuts

*Such a bright salad full of crunch, flavour and goodness – I'd love someone to make this
for my lunch every day! This is one of those substantial salads that seem to improve with
a little time so it's great to make when you're asked to bring something along. I would
also make it for a picnic or lunch party, and serve it with lamb chops or sausages.*

SERVES 6
PREP TIME : 20 MINS } COOK TIME : 15 MINS

1/2 cup (100 g) tri-colour quinoa
1/4 red cabbage, finely chopped (I use a mandolin)
2 crunchy red apples, thinly sliced
2 carrots, cut into matchsticks
1 bunch (about 500 g/1 lb 2 oz) radishes, cut into matchsticks
1 handful rocket (arugula)
1 cup (80 g) shaved parmesan cheese

Candied walnuts
2/3 cup (150 g) caster (superfine) sugar
3 cups (350 g) walnuts
1/2 tsp cayenne pepper
1/2 tsp fennel seeds

Tahini dressing
1/4 cup (65 g) tahini
Grated zest and juice of 1 orange
1/4 cup (60 ml) olive oil
1 Tbsp pure maple syrup

For the candied walnuts, preheat the oven to 180°C (350°F). Grease a large baking tray.
Combine the sugar and 1/4 cup (60 ml) cold water in a saucepan. Cook over medium–low
heat for about 5 minutes or until the sugar has dissolved and the mixture turns light golden.
Remove from the heat and, working quickly, add the walnuts and spices. Stir to combine,
then spread the mixture over the tray and pop it into the oven for 7 minutes or until the
nuts are golden. Break up the nuts, then leave to cool.

While the walnuts are cooking, prepare the quinoa according to the packet instructions.
Set aside until needed.

To make the tahini dressing, shake all the ingredients in a jar until combined, then season
to taste – does it need more acid or salt? Store in the fridge until needed.

Combine the red cabbage, apple, carrot, radish, rocket and cooked quinoa in a large bowl.
Toss with the tahini dressing and sprinkle the parmesan and candied walnuts over the top.

More ideas for working lunches

- Leftovers are your friend – use salmon or chicken to make the Roasted cherry tomato, salmon and yoghurt salad (page 123), or use chicken or turkey for the Chicken potato salad with salsa verde (page 127).

- Make up and pack a selection of goodies from the Mezze platter on page 94.

- Think about beautiful Mediterranean flavours and dishes that generally improve after a few hours in their dressing, like the Cannellini bean, olive and almond salad with mint dressing (page 69).

- Opt for salads that have a bit of protein and perhaps some noodles, rice, legumes or other whole grains to stretch the ingredients a bit further and make more than one lunch at a time.

- Use sturdy, chunky vegetables (like roasted cauliflower or broccoli) rather than leafy greens, which quickly wilt

RAINBOW PICKLE

There's so much to love about this little pickle, but the main thing is that it uses up a load of zucchini, which many of us have an overabundance of at this time of year (you turn your back on the garden for a minute and I swear they quadruple in size!). This is a 'fridge pickle' so, as the name suggests, do store it in the fridge.

MAKES ABOUT 5 CUPS
PREP TIME : 20 MINS, PLUS STANDING
COOK TIME : 5 MINS

5 cups (675 g) grated zucchini (courgette)
3 carrots, grated
1 red onion, finely diced
2 cups (400 g) corn kernels
1 cup (65 g) English spinach or chard stalks, finely chopped
1/4 cup (55 g) salt
2 cups (500 ml) apple cider vinegar
1 cup (220 g) sugar
1 Tbsp fennel seeds
1 Tbsp brown mustard seeds
1 tsp coriander seeds
1/2 tsp chilli flakes, or to taste

Combine all of the vegetables in a large bowl and use your hands to massage in the salt really well. Cover and set aside for an hour or two.

Combine the vinegar, sugar and spices in a small saucepan to make the brine. Bring to a simmer, then stir and cook for a few minutes until the sugar has dissolved. Set aside until needed.

Transfer the vegetables to a large colander and press out as much liquid as you can (you might need to do this in several batches). Divide the mixture among a few glass jars, filling them about four-fifths of the way with the vegetables. Pour in the hot brine to fill the jars. Seal tightly and wait for at least a day before using the pickle. The flavour will develop further over a week or so. Store the pickle in the fridge for up to 6 weeks.

Rainbow pickle and GRUYERE TOASTIES

Who doesn't love a toastie? You can use the rainbow pickle here or a good store-bought pickle. If you're taking this to work, prepare the sandwich at home, but put the pickle in a separate container and wrap the sandwich in baking paper. At lunchtime, just add the pickle to the sandwich and cook it in a hot sandwich press.

SERVES 6
PREP TIME : 10 MINS   COOK TIME : 5 MINS

12 thin slices wholemeal sourdough bread
Butter, for spreading
Rainbow pickle (see left)
6 slices gruyere or other mild, nutty cheese
Lemon wedges, to serve (optional)

Spread one side of each slice of bread with a little butter. Top the unbuttered sides of half the bread with a few tablespoons of the pickle and a slice of cheese each. Top with the remaining bread slices, buttered side up.

Cook the sandwiches in a hot sandwich press until golden brown. Serve with a sprinkle of sea salt and a squeeze of lemon, if you like.

Cacao, banana and peanut butter smoothie

Combine 2 Tbsp raw cacao powder, 1 sliced frozen banana, 1 1/2 cups (375 ml) milk or water, 2 pitted dates, 1 Tbsp peanut butter and 1 tsp chia seeds in a high-powered blender. Whizz until smooth. Chill until needed – just give it a good shake before drinking. *Serves 1*

SUMMER

Cheers to catching up with good friends over beautiful fresh food prepared with lots of love and served generously.

Long summer days are the perfect excuse for packing up a memorable dinner picnic to linger over and watch the sun going down.

Ice cream by the river; legs dangling in the cool water as the sun sinks and the heat of the day softens into a balmy summer's night. Heaven!

Sometimes a 'chatter platter' is the perfect dinner – lots of yummy food to graze on and it's made in advance so you can just enjoy being together and catching up.

The perfect summer picnic

This picnic haunts me. I think of it on the hottest days, when all I want to do is lie under a tree on some soft green grass, feast on these dishes and drink ice-cold rosé. And I fantasise about it on the coldest days, when that kind of heat feels impossible.

Full of flavour, texture, love and completely made in advance, this is an unforgettable, completely attainable meal to make and pack up to take somewhere special. The bottom of the garden, perhaps? Or the nature strip on your street, the beach, the back paddock or your kitchen bench?

I served this meal when I was catering for a group of artists that my mother (artist and teacher Annie Herron) took to Burgundy. We enjoyed a picnic lunch on the last day in a beautiful spot between vines and hills where Mum had parked everyone for a morning of sketching and watercolours. It was a lovely scene and the food delivered lots of flavour and colour and, I hope, a little joy.

How to make do when you're cooking in a holiday rental

- Keep it simple! As long as you have a few basics – good olive oil, butter, sea salt, lemons, chilli and garlic – you have the foundations of a top holiday meal.
- Be prepared to chuck out your meal plan and run with whatever is available. Find the local market or shopping strip and stock up on whatever looks good – buy the ingredients that get you excited and make them the star. If you have good produce, olive oil, one or two nice cheeses and lovely wine, you are all set.
- Roasting tins work well for baking cakes into big slab cakes and, at a pinch, so do saucepans and ovenproof frying pans. You might need to double the quantity from your original recipe.
- A cold bottle of rosé makes a great rolling pin for pastry... plus you get to drink it!
- The bottom of a glass is great for crushing up nuts or biscuits for a cheesecake base, or for pressing pastry into a tin.
- Here's a great picnic hack: keep your rosé icy cold by chilling it thoroughly, then pouring it into a large insulated water bottle. They keep liquids cold for up to 12 hours.

CANNELLINI BEAN, OLIVE *and* ALMOND SALAD *with mint dressing*
Walnut, mustard and CARAMELISED ONION TART
PEACH, PINE NUT *and* LAVENDER CAKE

Add some sliced cold meats, cheeses, dips and sliced baguette for a truly indulgent feast.

CANNELLINI BEAN, OLIVE *and* ALMOND SALAD *with mint dressing*

I always make a salad like this for a picnic, mostly because it stands up so well to transportation and 'sitting around for a bit', but also because it adds a bit of healthy sustenance to the meal, and can smoothly transition from tasty side dish to fancy bruschetta starter. I would definitely double this recipe if you want some good leftovers for lunches.

SERVES 6
PREP TIME : 15 MINS } COOK TIME : NIL

400 g (14 oz) tin cannellini beans, rinsed and drained,
   or 1 cup (195 g) dried cannellini beans, soaked overnight
   in cold water, then cooked until tender
1 cup (125 g) slivered almonds, toasted
2 telegraph cucumbers, chopped
1 handful radishes, quartered
1 cup (125 g) pitted green olives, halved

Mint dressing
1 handful mint leaves, plus extra to serve
2 Tbsp capers, rinsed
4 anchovy fillets
1 garlic clove, crushed
1 cup (250 ml) olive oil
Juice of 1 lemon, or to taste

Combine the cannellini beans, almonds, cucumber, radish and olives in a large bowl.

Whisk the dressing ingredients together and check for seasoning, adding a little more lemon juice if needed.

Pour the dressing over the salad and gently toss with your hands to combine – you don't want the beans to break up and turn to mush. Cover and keep in the fridge until needed.

About half an hour before serving, take the salad out of the fridge – the flavours will come alive at room temperature. Add the extra mint leaves to serve.

Walnut, mustard and
CARAMELISED ONION TART

Indulgent, yes (there's a fair amount of butter and cream here) – but completely delicious and always crowd-pleasing? One hundred per cent. This is a cracker of a recipe and not at all difficult, especially if you use store-bought pastry for the base (the tart will still be wonderful but the shell won't be quite as flaky and golden as if you'd made the pastry). I like to double this recipe to make two tarts, one for now and one for the freezer.

SERVES 6
PREP TIME : 30 MINS, PLUS CHILLING ⁀ COOK TIME : 1 HOUR

Rough puff pastry
250 g (9 oz) chilled butter, cut into cubes
1²/₃ cups (250 g) plain (all-purpose) flour,
    plus extra for dusting
¼ cup (60 ml) chilled water

Filling
2 Tbsp olive oil
3 brown onions, sliced
3 eggs
1 cup (250 ml) single (pure) cream
2 tsp wholegrain mustard
½ cup (50 g) grated Comte or gruyere cheese
1 cup (115 g) walnuts, lightly toasted and
    roughly chopped

To make the pastry, combine the butter and flour on the bench, using the heel of your hand to work them together. Add chilled water as necessary to form a rough dough – it's okay to see some marbled streaks of butter. Cover and chill in the fridge for 30 minutes.

Roll out the pastry on a lightly floured surface into a large rectangle. Dust off any loose flour. Fold the top half of the pastry down, then fold the bottom half up so you have a long slim rectangle. Turn the pastry 90 degrees and roll it into another large rectangle, rolling in one direction if possible (this helps keep your pastry nice and flaky). Fold and roll the pastry into another slim rectangle, then cover and chill for 20 minutes.

Roll out the pastry on a lightly floured surface until 3 mm (⅛ inch) thick. Gently drape the pastry over a 36 x 11 cm (14¼ x 4¼ inch) loose-based rectangular tart tin and trim the edges. Return to the fridge for 30 minutes. Preheat the oven to 180°C (350°F).

To make the filling, heat the olive oil in a heavy-based saucepan over medium heat. Cook the onion, stirring often, for about 20 minutes or until golden and completely caramelised.

Meanwhile, line the pastry with baking paper and fill the base with pastry weights, uncooked rice or dried beans (this stops the base rising during baking). Bake for 20 minutes. Remove the weights and paper and bake for another 10 minutes or until the pastry is pale and dry.

Combine the eggs, cream, mustard, cheese and a good pinch of sea salt in a bowl and whisk well. Scatter the caramelised onion over the pastry base, sprinkle with the walnuts, then gently pour in the egg mixture so it comes three-quarters of the way up the sides of the shell. Bake the tart for about 30 minutes or until the pastry is golden and the filling is just set.

Recipe pictured page 73, top right

PEACH, PINE NUT
and LAVENDER CAKE

This cake is my love note to France in the summer – a happy combination of lavender,
pine nuts, peaches, honey and that wonderful French butter that pops with little crystals
of sea salt. It's an ambrosial flavour combination and one of my all-time favourite cakes,
especially when served at a picnic with fresh cherries and plenty of rosé or sparkling
wine on hand.

I usually make this in a large roasting tin so you end up with more of a slab cake, but
you could absolutely cook it in a large round cake tin if you prefer. Or halve the quantities
and make it in a smaller cake tin or a square slice tin.

SERVES 8–10
PREP TIME : 15 MINS 〉 COOK TIME : ABOUT 1 HOUR

8 peaches, halved
1½ cups (330 g) caster (superfine) sugar
375 g (13 oz) butter, softened
Grated zest of 1 lemon
6 eggs
1¼ cups (125 g) almond meal
2 cups (300 g) plain (all-purpose) flour
1½ tsp baking powder
¼ cup (90 g) honey
3 Tbsp fresh or dried lavender
½ cup (80 g) pine nuts, toasted

Preheat the oven to 220°C (425°F). Grease a large roasting tin – mine is about 60 x 40 cm
(24 x 16 inches). Line the tin and a baking tray with baking paper.

Put the peach halves on the tray and sprinkle with about ½ cup (110 g) of the sugar. Bake for
15 minutes or until the peaches are caramelised on top and beginning to soften.

Reduce the oven temperature to 180°C (350°F).

Meanwhile, put the butter, remaining sugar and lemon zest in the bowl of an electric mixer
and beat until pale and fluffy. Add the eggs, one at a time, beating well after each addition.
In a separate bowl, whisk together the almond meal, flour and baking powder, then fold this
mixture into the creamed butter and sugar.

Spoon the batter into the roasting tin. Arrange the peach halves on top and drizzle with the
honey. Sprinkle the lavender and pine nuts over the top. Bake the cake for 35–40 minutes
or until golden and cooked through. Leave the cake in the tin to carry to your picnic and
serve warm or at room temperature.

Recipe pictured page 73, bottom left

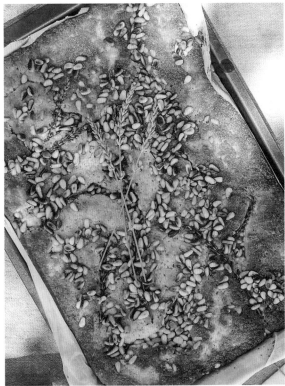

New Year's Eve for your nearest and dearest

Sometimes you want to go all out for New Year's Eve. And other times you just want to sit around a table in the garden with your absolute favourite people, light some candles, pour a glass of the best wine and have a delicious meal with no pressure, no crowds and no queues.

This was our table last New Year's Eve and I remember it as being one of the best meals of my whole life – the perfect way to ring in a new year.

This is a special-occasion meal, but that's not to say that you couldn't (and shouldn't!) make the truffles to give to a friend having a shocker of a week, or do the chicken on any old Monday night; actually, it would be such an easy, throw-together weeknight meal, we should all add it to the list. But when each of these recipes and elements come together, at a table set with candles and flowers, and preferably in the garden under a soft summer sky, it's my idea of perfection.

Making a small, special dinner for just a few people is something I love to do. No pressure, no need to create huge quantities of anything, just a table set prettily and two or three simple things to place on it and share.

More ideas for little 'menus'

- Julie Delpy-style chicken with calvados and crème fraîche (page 33), then Walnut and fennel biscotti (page 151)
- Greek salad with chicken, risoni and caramelised lemon (page 57), then Fig and almond cake (page 165)
- Fish pie (page 181) with Pickle salad (page 182), then Chocolate bark (page 250)
- Amaro spritz (page 186), Roasted eye fillet with quince glaze (page 249), then Chocolate, hazelnut and espresso cake (page 36)
- Barbecued lamb shoulder with whipped feta and pistachio crumbs (page 25) and Jewelled rice pilaf (page 22), then Annabelle's quince and pecan ice cream (page 190)

VODKA SOUR COCKTAILS
Crunchy DOUBLE-COOKED POTATOES
Garlic, honey and rosemary ROASTED CHICKEN PIECES
BEARNAISE SAUCE ❧ CRUNCHY SALAD
PRALINE TRUFFLES

New Year's Eve with my absolute favourite people, in the garden under a soft summer sky, is my idea of perfection.

Vodka sour cocktails

A few hours before dinner, make a sugar syrup by combining 1 cup (220 g) sugar with 3 cups (750 ml) water in a saucepan. Bring to a simmer over medium heat, stirring to dissolve the sugar. You could add a vanilla bean, a cinnamon stick, some fresh rosemary or thyme, or some lemon zest and juice, to taste, or just keep it simple. Pour the syrup into a jar and place it in the fridge to cool completely.

For each person, mix 1 shot (30 ml/1 fl oz) of vodka (or to taste) with the same quantity of sugar syrup, a good squeeze of lemon juice and plenty of ice in a glass. Top up with mineral water or soda water and a few fresh raspberries.

For a non-alcoholic version, simply leave out the vodka.

Crunchy DOUBLE-COOKED POTATOES

A big bowl of golden, crunchy potatoes is a welcome sight to all. Especially when it's sitting pretty next to a platter of honey-roasted chicken and served with home-made bearnaise sauce. YUM. And if you don't already par-boil your potatoes before roasting them, then please start! It makes such a big, crunchy difference.

SERVES 6–8

PREP TIME : 10 MINS 〉 COOK TIME : ABOUT 1¼ HOURS

1 kg (2 lb 4 oz) baby potatoes, halved
¼ cup (60 ml) olive oil

Preheat the oven to 220°C (425°F).

Put the potatoes in a large saucepan of water. Bring to the boil over high heat and cook until the potatoes are just tender when pierced with a fork. Drain the potatoes in a colander and shake them around to slightly roughen up the edges.

Tip the potatoes into a roasting tin and use the base of a glass to smash/flatten each potato just a little. Drizzle with the olive oil and sprinkle with some salt and pepper. Cook until the potatoes are golden and crunchy, about 45 minutes to 1 hour.

Garlic, honey and rosemary
ROASTED CHICKEN PIECES

Anyone who knows me knows I'm mad for a tray bake – the kind of meal you can just throw together in one big pan and pop into the oven to do its thing while you have drinks. Combining flavours like this in the one tray, in a hot oven, really does create a caramelised magic that's a hands-down crowd-pleaser. Plus, because the chicken is already jointed, you don't even need to carve it. Just transfer it to a platter and add a jug of Bearnaise sauce and a fresh Crunchy salad (see right), plus the roasted potatoes from page 77.

SERVES 8

PREP TIME : 20 MINS ❯ COOK TIME : 1¹⁄₂ HOURS

2 chickens, jointed into 6 pieces each
8 garlic cloves
2 Tbsp rosemary leaves
2 Tbsp thyme leaves
1 tsp salt
2 Tbsp honey
Juice of 2 lemons
2–3 Tbsp boiling water
2 Tbsp dijon mustard
¹⁄₃ cup (80 ml) olive oil
1 cup (250 ml) white wine
¹⁄₄ cup (60 ml) boiling water, extra

Preheat the oven to 220°C (425°F). Put the chicken in a deep-sided baking tray, large enough that the pieces don't overlap.

Put the garlic, rosemary, thyme and salt on your chopping board and finely chop everything together so you have a garlicky herb paste. In a small bowl, combine the honey, lemon juice and enough boiling water to help thin the honey a little. Whisk together, then add the mustard and olive oil, scrape in your herb paste and whisk again.

Rub the garlic herb mixture all over the chicken pieces so that each one gets a good coating. Bake for 20 minutes or until the chicken is beginning to brown and caramelise. Pour 200 ml (7 fl oz) of the wine over the chicken. Reduce the heat to 150°C (300°F) and bake the chicken for 1 hour or until cooked through (check one of the thickest pieces).

Transfer the chicken pieces to a large serving platter and cover with foil. Scrape every last piece of anything stuck to the base of your baking tray into a small saucepan. Pour in the roasting juices and the remaining wine and bring to a simmer. Pour in the extra ¹⁄₄ cup (60 ml) boiling water and bring to the boil, cooking until the mixture reduces to a lovely flavoursome sauce. Pour the sauce over the chicken and serve.

Recipe pictured page 76

BEARNAISE SAUCE

This recipe comes from my late grandmother, Helen, who was wonderful at making all the classic sauces. Yes, it has a crazy amount of butter, but a little goes a long way and it's just so delicious! I love it most with this crispy roast chicken and potato feast, but it's also excellent, of course, with roast beef. Come springtime, a platter of blanched asparagus scattered with toasted slivered almonds and a bowl of bearnaise on the side makes one of the loveliest lunches you can imagine.

MAKES ABOUT 1 CUP (250 ML)
PREP TIME : 10 MINS ⟩ COOK TIME : 15 MINS

²/₃ cup (170 ml) white wine vinegar
1 tsp lemon juice, or to taste
1 French shallot, finely diced
1 tsp freshly ground black pepper
1 bunch tarragon
3 egg yolks
250 g (9 oz) butter, cut into cubes

Put the vinegar, lemon juice, shallot and pepper in a small saucepan. Add all but a few of the tarragon leaves and bring to the boil. Reduce the heat and simmer for about 5 minutes so the liquid reduces by about half. Remove from the heat and set aside to cool.

Pour enough water into a small saucepan to come about a quarter of the way up the side and bring to a simmer. Pour the vinegar mixture into a heatproof glass bowl and sit it on top of the pan of simmering water. Whisk in the egg yolks and keep whisking until the mixture thickens, about 5 minutes. (Gran had one of those hand-held electric whisks that she would use to make this and I do the same, although you can easily whisk it yourself if you have the muscle power.)

Slowly beat in the butter, a little at a time, whisking slowly as the mixture emulsifies and being careful not to overheat and curdle the eggs. Once all of the butter has been added and the sauce is lovely and thick, test for flavour – it may need a little more lemon juice or some salt. Add the reserved tarragon leaves and either serve straight away or transfer it to a jar and keep it in the fridge for up to 3 days.

Crunchy salad

A meal like this needs a light, bright crunchy salad. I just chop up a big iceberg lettuce, throw in some chopped radishes and cucumber and then toss it with a dressing of Salsa verde (page 15) thinned out with a little olive oil.

PRALINE TRUFFLES

By the time dessert rolls around with a dinner like this, the last thing you want to do is leave the table to plate up a cake or pudding. Because isn't this the very best part of a meal? Everyone is replete and happy, the conversation is flowing and life is good — especially when you can just fling the dishes into the sink to think about later, take the truffles out of the fridge and pop another bottle of bubbles.

This recipe is my ode to the crunchy toffee and milk chocolate truffles that did my cheeks no favours when I lived in Paris in my early twenties. They came wrapped in red and gold foil and were sold at every tabac in town. Thankfully, I suppose, I've never seen them in Australia. For special dinners, I make up a batch and then try to keep them well away from my greedy little fingers until after dinner.

MAKES 12–15
PREP TIME : 30 MINS } COOK TIME : 30 MINS

400 g (14 oz) milk chocolate, chopped
1 cup (250 ml) thick (double) cream
2 Tbsp (40 g) butter
A pinch of salt
1/2 tsp vanilla extract

Hazelnut praline
1 cup (135 g) hazelnuts
1 cup (220 g) caster (superfine) sugar

To make the praline, preheat the oven to 180°C (350°F). Scatter the hazelnuts onto a baking tray. Bake for 10–15 minutes or until the nuts are golden and smelling delicious. Tip the nuts into a clean tea towel and rub them to remove as much of the skin as possible, then tip into a colander and shake away any skin. Don't worry if there's a little skin on some of the hazelnuts. Tip the nuts onto a chopping board or into a food processor and chop fairly finely. Spread the chopped nuts over a baking tray lined with baking paper.

Put the sugar in a small heavy-based saucepan over medium heat. Cook, swirling the pan around every now and then, until the sugar has melted into a golden toffee (watch carefully as it can burn very quickly!). Remove from the heat and pour the toffee over the chopped hazelnuts. Set aside until the toffee sets, then use a large sharp knife or a food processor to chop the praline into coarse crumbs.

Put 250 g (9 oz) of the chopped chocolate in a heatproof glass bowl. Pour the cream into a small saucepan and bring just to boiling point. Whisk in the butter, salt and vanilla, then remove from the heat. Pour the cream mixture over the chocolate and stir until melted.

Reserve a few tablespoons of the praline for decorating. Stir the remaining praline into the chocolate mixture. Cover and place in the fridge to cool and set for 1 hour.

Line a baking tray with baking paper. Roll the chocolate mixture into small balls about the size of a walnut. Arrange on the tray, then return to the fridge to firm up again.

Meanwhile, melt the remaining chocolate in a heatproof glass bowl set over a saucepan of simmering water. Using two forks or a toothpick, dunk each truffle into the chocolate and then return it to the tray. Sprinkle the truffles with the reserved praline, then return to the fridge to set.

CHATTER PLATTERS

All hail the chatter platter! A great big, generous platter of good things to graze on all evening is a perfectly acceptable alternative to a sit-down dinner. And actually, it can be more conducive to good chats and nice times because nobody is rushing to and from the kitchen to serve, scrape, rinse, wipe down the bench or whatever.

Next time you're hosting book club, the girls for Friday night drinks or the neighbours for a casual catch up, just load up a big board or basket with some of the recipes on the following pages, plonk it down on the table for everyone to serve themselves and get on with the really good part of having friends over: talking to them over good food!

If you fancy finishing the night with something sweet, why not stick with the theme and serve a big platter of fresh fruit with some Chocolate bark (page 250)?

More ideas for chatter platters

· Fiona's olive oil crackers (page 48) with goat's cheese and pickles
· Deconstructed Niçoise platter (page 102) with some fresh bread rolls
· Salmon rillettes (page 110) with Garlic toasted sourdough (page 85)
· Little herb pies with pickles (page 144), perhaps with Pistachio and mint tapenade (page 97) and some chopped vegetables
· No-need-to-knead focaccia squares (page 187) with goat's curd and honeycomb
· Caramelised fennel and brie dip (page 246) with crusty bread
· A selection of yummy store-bought dips and cheeses (the point is actually getting people together, so if you don't have time this Friday to do any of the above, send that text invite anyway and pop into your local deli for help with the food)

BRUSCHETTA PLATTER
CHEESE PLATTER
MEZZE PLATTER

I love entertaining with one big platter of goodness!

BRUSCHETTA PLATTER

GARLIC TOASTED SOURDOUGH

Warm STREAKY BACON, BLUE CHEESE *and* FIGS

TOMATO, ROCKMELON *and* HOT-SMOKED TROUT

Chargrilled ZUCCHINI *and* NASTURTIUM PESTO

ARANCINI

This is my idea of heaven for a warm summer's evening, but it works just as well for brunch: loads of crusty, garlicky, toasted sourdough with a few different topping options (or even just one). On this particular occasion we sat under an elm tree at sunset with wine and a couple of beers, and also a batch of golden fried arancini (because everyone loves fried stuff, especially with drinks!).

The tree and garden belong to artist Harriet Goodall, a friend from school days and now an artist living in the Southern Highlands of New South Wales. Harriet creates the most beautiful woven sculptures and it is always a joy to sneak into her studio and catch up with her, her husband Mat (who manages farm properties and is an amazing cook himself), and their children, Banjo and Clementine. Their house is full of curiosities, style and creativity, and their garden, where we shared this chatter platter, is a divine place to spend a few hours.

Harriet's bag of tricks when having guests

- We always have the outside fire going, with cushions and blankets on all the chairs for pre-dinner drinks and post-dinner chats. I like to move people around a little.

- Music is such a scene-setter, so I have playlists all ready to rev things up or settle them down.

- We have sets of string lights in a box in the cupboard, ready to hang in the trees – it's such an easy way to make things feel fun and festive.

- Our friends all like to bring something to contribute – a salad, some nibbles, a cake – and I let them!

- When it comes to food, we generally plonk everything on big serving plates on the table or side table for people to help themselves, rather than plating up individual serves. It's convivial, it really takes the pressure off getting everyone to the table, and there's no pressure to eat things on your plate just to be polite.

- I always have a no-cook dessert.

- We usually ask people to come before sunset so we can have a walk around with a drink and see the garden and the animals, and if we party on, we mostly still finish early.

- We do the dishes before we go to bed. Every time. It's a good chance to debrief and makes the morning sleep-in all the sweeter.

@harrietgoodallartist

Garlic toasted sourdough

Preheat the oven to 180°C (350°F). Slice half a
day-old loaf of sourdough bread and arrange the
slices on two lined baking trays. Drizzle the bread
with ¼ cup (60 ml) olive oil. Pop the trays into
the oven until the bread is just turning golden
(don't let it go too far or it will become brittle).

As soon as you remove the trays from the oven,
rub each slice of bread with the cut side of a garlic
clove (you'll need 4 garlic cloves) and sprinkle with
sea salt flakes. Serve the toasted sourdough warm
or let it cool completely and store it in an airtight
container for a couple of days. *Serves 6*

Warm STREAKY BACON, BLUE CHEESE *and* FIGS

This is probably my favourite of all three bruschetta toppings, but that's because I don't think you can go past warm figs, blue cheese and bacon all together on crusty bread.

SERVES 4–6
PREP TIME : 5 MINS ⟩ COOK TIME : 20 MINS

200 g (7 oz) streaky bacon
6 figs, quartered
200 g (7 oz) blue cheese, crumbled

Preheat the oven to 180°C (350°F). Put the bacon on a baking tray and cook for 10 minutes or until almost cooked to your liking. Push the bacon to one side of the tray, add the fig pieces and cook for another 5 minutes. Add the cheese and pop the tray back into the oven for a few minutes until the cheese is just softened. Combine the mixture in a bowl and serve with toasted sourdough.

TOMATO, ROCKMELON *and* HOT-SMOKED TROUT

If you're serving this chatter platter for brunch, you could also add some poached eggs to the tomato mixture.

SERVES 6
PREP TIME : 10 MINS ⟩ COOK TIME : NIL

250 g (9 oz) hot-smoked trout
500 g (1 lb 2 oz) heirloom tomatoes, cut into chunks
1/2 rockmelon, cut into cubes
1 scant handful basil leaves
2 Tbsp extra virgin olive oil
Grated zest and juice of 1 lemon
1 tsp ground sumac

Flake the trout into a bowl and combine with the tomato, rockmelon and basil. Dress with the olive oil, lemon zest, lemon juice, sumac and a little salt and freshly ground black pepper to taste. Pile the mixture into a bowl and serve with toasted sourdough.

Chargrilled ZUCCHINI *and* NASTURTIUM PESTO

If you happen to have nasturtium growing in your garden, you probably have lots of it – even I, with my black thumbs, can grow it in abundance. So when I came across the idea of nasturtium pesto, I was on board! It has a peppery, fresh flavour that goes beautifully with the mellow zucchini. You can swap the nasturtium with basil for a traditional pesto.

SERVES 6
PREP TIME : 10 MINS COOK TIME : 5–10 MINS

5 zucchini (courgettes), cut into long thin strips
1/4 cup (60 ml) olive oil
Lemon juice, to taste
2–3 nasturtium flowers
Mint leaves, to serve

Nasturtium pesto
1 cup (50 g) nasturtium leaves
4 mint leaves
2 garlic cloves, roughly chopped
6 nasturtium seed pods
1/2 cup (80 g) pine nuts, toasted
1/2 cup (45 g) grated parmesan or pecorino cheese
Grated zest and juice of 1 lemon
1/2 cup (125 ml) olive oil, plus extra for storing
1/2 tsp sea salt

For the pesto, combine all the ingredients in a blender or food processor and blitz until the pesto has a nice thick consistency. Taste and add more salt, lemon juice or cheese if needed. Spoon the pesto into a glass jar and seal with a little extra olive oil, then keep it in the fridge until needed.

Preheat a chargrill pan or barbecue on high. Drizzle the zucchini with the olive oil and cook, turning once, for a couple of minutes on each side or until golden. Transfer to a bowl, then toss the warm zucchini with a few tablespoons of the pesto, a good squeeze of lemon juice, some nasturtium flowers and mint leaves. Serve with toasted sourdough.

Recipes pictured page 85

ARANCINI

I know that the idea of frying food can seem like way too much trouble when friends come over. But bear with me, because actually it's not (assuming we're talking about a group of around eight people – any more and it gets too time consuming and you'll miss all the fun).

Arancini are a great option because you can cook them before anyone arrives and then reheat them in a really hot oven when needed. Or if it's just for a handful of friends, have the arancini ready in the fridge and fry them to order.

MAKES ABOUT 20
PREP TIME : 30 MINS, PLUS CHILLING ❳ COOK TIME : 40 MINS

2 Tbsp olive oil
1 brown onion, diced
1¹/2 cups (330 g) arborio rice
¹/2 cup (125 ml) white wine
4 cups (1 litre) warm chicken or vegetable
    stock or water
¹/2 cup (45 g) grated parmesan cheese

1¹/2 Tbsp (30 g) butter
2 cups (220 g) dry breadcrumbs
3 eggs
Vegetable oil, for deep-frying
Aioli, Salsa verde (page 15) or
    sea salt flakes, to serve

Heat the olive oil in a large heavy-based frying pan over medium heat. Cook the onion for about 5 minutes or until translucent. Add the rice and stir so every grain is coated with a little oil, then add the wine and cook for a minute or so, stirring as you go.

Stir a cupful of the stock or water into the rice and keep stirring until the liquid is nearly all absorbed. Repeat with the remaining stock or water, adding a cupful at a time and stirring until it is all absorbed into the rice, which should now be al dente. Remove from the heat, stir in the parmesan and butter and pop it into the fridge to chill.

Line a baking tray with baking paper, tip the breadcrumbs into a bowl and whisk the eggs in another bowl. Scoop up a little rice and roll it into a ball about the size of a walnut or golf ball, depending on how big you want your arancini to be. Roll the ball in the egg and then coat it with the breadcrumbs. Place on the tray and repeat with the remaining rice. Place the balls in the fridge for at least half an hour before frying.

Preheat the oven to 160°C (320°F). Heat the vegetable oil in a large saucepan over high heat until it reaches 180°C (350°F) or until a little piece of bread instantly bubbles and sizzles up to the surface of the oil. Fry the arancini in batches until golden brown all over.

Return the arancini to the lined tray and pop them into the oven for 10 minutes so they are all warm. Serve with aioli, salsa verde or just a good sprinkling of sea salt.

Variations

- PEA: Stir a handful of cooked peas through the chilled rice before rolling into balls.

- MOZZARELLA: Push a small piece of mozzarella into each ball of rice and squeeze together so the cheese is completely encased in the rice.

- RAGU: If you have left-over ragu or a lovely rich bolognese sauce handy, push a small amount into the rice balls as for the mozzarella.

CHEESE PLATTER

Cheese

Prosciutto

OLIVE *and* HAZELNUT TAPENADE

Witlof

Fresh honeycomb

Fresh figs

Roasted hazelnuts

Bread

PEACH *and* ROSEMARY G&T

A cheese platter is always a good thing – either with drinks, for dinner itself or after dinner. My Danish grandfather would often have his version of a cheese platter for breakfast: a big hunk of gouda cheese, an egg, a few crackers and maybe a tomato or some radishes.

The point I'm trying to make is that everyone loves a cheese platter, especially when it's done right. Here are a few tips from an expert on this front – cheesemaker Cressida Cains of Pecora Dairy in Robertson, New South Wales.

Cressida's tips for a great cheese platter

- Try to buy something local.
- Think about the milk the cheeses are produced from – often providing a sheep or goat cheese will cater for any dietary requirements your guests may have.
- A hard, soft and blue are a traditional mix on a cheese platter, but go with what you love or what might pair well with the accompaniments that you already have or enjoy eating.
- Don't worry too much about rules – just make it generous and have a variety of different textures of both cheese and pairings.
- Consider cutting up some of the cheese to get people started. It can be intimidating to be the first to slice into a little wheel or chunk of cheese.
- I think that cheese is for every day. Don't save it for best – it's such an important source of calcium and protein, so just buy it and eat it!

@pecoradairy

OLIVE *and* HAZELNUT TAPENADE

This rough tapenade will come in deliciously handy in so many different ways. On a cheese platter it adds crunch, tang and loads of flavour, but it's also lovely tossed through pasta or served with roast lamb. It makes a great bruschetta topping and would also be beautiful with the Arancini on page 89.

MAKES ABOUT 2 CUPS
PREP TIME : 10 MINS ❧ COOK TIME : NIL

2 cups (300 g) pitted green and black olives, finely chopped
1/2 cup (75 g) toasted hazelnuts, chopped
8 anchovy fillets, drained and roughly chopped
2 garlic cloves, finely chopped
2 Tbsp capers, rinsed and finely chopped
1 handful parsley leaves, roughly chopped
1 tsp lemon thyme leaves
Grated zest and juice of 1 lemon
2 Tbsp olive oil
2 tsp red wine vinegar
Chilli flakes, to taste

Mix all the ingredients together in a bowl until well combined. Check the seasoning and adjust to taste.

Peach and rosemary G&T

For each person, pour 1 shot (30 ml/1 fl oz) of gin (or to taste) into a glass with plenty of ice. Add a few slices of ripe peach, a sprig of rosemary and a squeeze of lime. Top up with tonic water. You can also make this in a jug to suit the number of guests and serve it over ice.

MEZZE PLATTER

MERGUEZ MEATBALLS *with hummus*

PISTACHIO *and* MINT TAPENADE

BAKED FETA *and* OLIVES

SLOW-ROASTED TOMATOES *and* EGGPLANT

Cucumber batons

SIMPLE DUKKAH *and chilli flakes on hard-boiled eggs*

Zataar-baked PITA CHIPS

This platter would be beautiful for a grazing dinner or as a substantial starter for a crowd. Having friends over doesn't get any easier than this – everything is done and plated up in advance so that all you need to do is deliver it to the table and relax with your guests.

My tips for creating a beautiful mezze platter

- Roast a load of vegetables and make this the centrepiece of your platter – it's an affordable and delicious way to add colour and substance.

- Home-made pita chips cost a fraction of the store-bought ones (and I also think they're much tastier).

- If you're short on time, stock up on store-bought dips and jazz them up with a sprinkle of dukkah, a swirl of pomegranate molasses or some chopped nuts and herbs.

- Pile the elements into a large basket or onto a platter and try to make it look as abundant and generous as possible. We eat first with our eyes and a beautiful bright mezze platter is a sure-fire way to please everyone.

- It's nice to add something a bit more substantial like the meatballs here, but you could also use chicken skewers, little lamb pies or store-bought pastizzi pastries.

MERGUEZ MEATBALLS *with hummus*

These little flavour bombs are beautiful in a mezze platter such as this, but also for dinner when served with some pearl couscous, yoghurt, extra harissa sauce and a cucumber and tomato salsa sprinkled with sumac.

SERVES 4–6 AS PART OF A MEZZE PLATTER
PREP TIME : 15 MINS ⸙ COOK TIME : 20 MINS

500 g (1 lb 2 oz) lamb mince
3 garlic cloves, finely chopped
1 Tbsp harissa, or to taste
1 Tbsp tomato paste (concentrated purée)
1 tsp sweet paprika

1/2 tsp cumin seeds
1/2 tsp coriander seeds
1/2 tsp fennel seeds
Chopped parsley, for sprinkling
Hummus, to serve

Preheat the oven to 200°C (400°F). Line a baking tray with baking paper.

Using your hands, combine all the ingredients in a large bowl. Roll the mixture into walnut-sized balls and place on the tray. Bake the meatballs for 20 minutes or until cooked through. Serve warm or at room temperature, sprinkled with parsley and with hummus for dipping.

PISTACHIO *and* MINT TAPENADE

Loaded with big, bright flavour and super versatile, a jar of this tapenade in the fridge is a very handy thing to have. I stir it through rice or couscous, spread it over salmon fillets before blasting them in a hot oven for about 6 minutes or, as per this platter, use it as a dip for boiled eggs or veggies.

MAKES ABOUT 1 1/2 CUPS
PREP TIME : 10 MINS ⸙ COOK TIME : NIL

1/2 cup (80 g) almonds
1/2 cup (75 g) pepitas (pumpkin seeds)
1 cup (150 g) unsalted pistachios
1 handful parsley leaves, roughly chopped
1 handful mint leaves, roughly chopped
2 garlic cloves, finely chopped
Grated zest and juice of 1 lemon
1/2 cup (125 ml) olive oil

Combine all the ingredients with a mortar and pestle to make a coarse paste (or blitz them in a food processor). Season to taste.

BAKED FETA *and* OLIVES

Something magical happens to feta when it's baked with olives, lemon, garlic and rosemary. It becomes a creamy, soft flavour bomb that's gorgeous as part of a mezze platter or served on its own with crackers or toasted sourdough (see page 85).

SERVES 4–6 AS PART OF A MEZZE PLATTER
PREP TIME : 10 MINS 〉 COOK TIME : 15 MINS

280 g (10 oz) feta cheese
1 cup (175 g) mixed olives
1 lemon, cut into quarters
2 garlic cloves, unpeeled
1 rosemary stalk
1/4 cup (60 ml) olive oil

Preheat the oven to 180°C (350°F).

Put the feta in a small roasting tin and surround it with the olives and lemon quarters. Bruise the garlic cloves with the flat of a knife and add them to the tin. Strip the rosemary leaves from the stalk and sprinkle them over the feta. Drizzle the olive oil over the top and bake for 15 minutes or until the feta is soft and the whole lot is deliciously aromatic.

SLOW-ROASTED TOMATOES *and* EGGPLANT

Slow roasting vegetables creates beautiful, intense flavours. I buy loads of tomatoes and eggplant at this time of year to roast and then stash them in a jar in the fridge to smoosh over bruschetta or through pasta. Such a good, easy and cheap flavour bomb!

SERVES 4–6 AS PART OF A MEZZE PLATTER
PREP TIME : 5 MINS 〉 COOK TIME : 1 HOUR

8 roma tomatoes
Olive oil, for drizzling
6 long thin eggplants (aubergine) or 4 small globe-shaped eggplants

Preheat the oven to 150°C (300°F). Halve the tomatoes and place them on a baking tray. Drizzle with olive oil and sprinkle with lots of salt and freshly ground black pepper. Roast for 1 hour or until the tomatoes are completely collapsed and intensely flavoured.

Prepare and cook the eggplants in the same way, but reduce the cooking time to 40 minutes (increase the cooking time if using larger eggplants).

SIMPLE DUKKAH

It's a good idea to have a great dukkah recipe that you can use to pep up pretty much any simple dish. I love sprinkling dukkah on boiled or scrambled eggs, or just dipping warm bread into olive oil and then a little dish of dukkah.

MAKES ABOUT 1¹/₂ CUPS
PREP TIME : 5 MINS ⟩ COOK TIME : 10 MINS

¹/₂ cup (75 g) hazelnuts, toasted
¹/₂ cup (80 g) almonds, toasted
1 tsp sea salt
¹/₃ cup (50 g) sesame seeds
1 Tbsp coriander seeds
2 Tbsp cumin seeds

Place the hazelnuts and almonds in a food processor or mortar and pestle with the salt.

Combine the sesame, coriander and cumin seeds in a frying pan and toast until fragrant and the sesame seeds are golden. Add to the nut mix and blitz or bash to combine into roughish crumbs. Once cool, store in a clean jar for up to a month.

Zataar-baked PITA CHIPS

Baked pita chips are the best – so much cheaper than any store-bought cracker and much yummier, too. I've sprinkled them with zataar, but you could go old school and spread a little butter and Vegemite over the pita pieces and bake them until crisp. My gran always had an ice-cream container full of these snacks when we visited and I loved them so much.

SERVES 4–6 AS PART OF A MEZZE PLATTER
PREP TIME : 10 MINS ⟩ COOK TIME : 10 MINS

4 pita breads
Zataar, for sprinkling
Olive oil, for drizzling

Preheat the oven to 180°C (350°F). Cut each pita bread into small pieces about the size of corn chips. Scatter the bread pieces on a couple of baking trays, sprinkle with the zataar and drizzle with olive oil.

Cook for about 10 minutes or until the pita chips arc golden brown (keep a fairly close eye on them as golden brown can turn to dark burnt brown very quickly!). Once cool, store in an airtight container until needed.

Recipes pictured page 95

'Too hot to cook' summer lunch

You know when it's so oppressively hot that you can't bear even the idea of turning on the oven… but you want to see your friends or you have a crowd coming over and would like to feed them something very tasty? Here's your menu!

The dishes you see on these pages were enjoyed in a beautiful old chateau on a recent trip to Burgundy. When I wasn't pinching myself to be staying somewhere so incredible, I was cooking for a group of art students that my mum, Annie Herron, had brought to France for a week of painting, sketching, learning and eating. We had all the elements for a wonderful week in one of the most intoxicating parts of the world, but nature brought one more to the party: a crazy heatwave that kept temperatures in the high thirties pretty much 24 hours a day. This was fine for the most part – there was a pool and plenty of shady spots for our artists. But their poor cook (*moi!*) found her tiny kitchen quite the hot spot.

I looked to recipes that required minimum cooking and delivered maximum flavour and enjoyment. Here they are, ready for the next time you find yourself needing to feed people when it's too hot to consider using the oven after 8am.

Deconstructed NIÇOISE PLATTER ❧ *Crusty bread*
Gran's ALMOND CAKE ❧ *Fresh seasonal berries*

*When it's so hot that you can't bear the idea of
turning on the oven, look to recipes that need minimum cooking
and deliver maximum flavour.*

Deconstructed
NIÇOISE PLATTER

This one is less of a recipe and more of an assembly job and, I think, a delicious way to feed lots of people on a hot day. All you need is one big platter and plenty of good crusty bread.

Mayonnaise is very easy to make at home – you just need to put in a bit of elbow work (or co-opt those around you to take turns at whisking). You can also make it in a blender or food processor, but I find that by the time I've got the machine out, used it, washed it and put it away again, it's much easier just to whisk it by hand. Even easier again... just use a good-quality store-bought mayo and trick it up a bit by adding lemon juice or dijon mustard to taste. I tend to use a lighter olive oil in this as the flavour can be quite strong. You could also use half vegetable oil and half olive oil.

SERVES 6
PREP TIME : 35 MINS } COOK TIME : 15 MINS

1 kg (2 lb 4 oz) baby new potatoes
1/4 cup (60 ml) extra virgin olive oil
2 Tbsp capers, rinsed
Grated zest of 1 lemon
1 handful parsley leaves, finely chopped
    (optional)
2 garlic cloves, peeled
1 cup (175 g) marinated mixed olives
500 g (1 lb 2 oz) really good tinned tuna
    in oil, drained
12 hard-boiled eggs, halved
1–2 bunches radishes, halved if large
2 handfuls green beans, halved and
    blanched

Mayonnaise
3 egg yolks
1 Tbsp dijon mustard
2 garlic cloves, crushed
A good pinch of sea salt
1 cup (250 ml) olive oil

Cook the potatoes in a large saucepan of boiling water until they are completely tender when pierced with a skewer or fork, then drain. Toss the warm potatoes with the olive oil, capers and lemon zest, and season with sea salt and pepper. Once they've cooled down, gently toss in the parsley, if using.

For the mayonnaise, whisk together the egg yolks, mustard, garlic and sea salt until really well combined. Add the olive oil in a steady stream, whisking all the time so the mixture emulsifies and thickens as you go. Keep drizzling and whisking until all the oil has been added. If the mixture splits, just give it an extra good whisking and it should come back together. Store in the fridge until needed (it will thicken further after chilling for a while).

Rub the base of your serving platter with the garlic cloves (this might sound superfluous but it truly does make a subtle difference). Place the olives in a small bowl. Arrange the olives, tuna, eggs, radishes, beans and potatoes on the platter. (I've gone for a pin-wheel look, but feel free to gently mix everything together if you prefer.)

Serve with the mayonnaise and some crusty bread on the side and plenty of chilled rosé.

Gran's ALMOND CAKE

I included this recipe in my first book, Local is Lovely, *but it's too good not to share here as well – this recipe is my family's gift to you, or rather my grandmother's gift. It's the perfect 'pudding cake' in the sense that it's delicate and pretty enough to serve with berries and cream as a dessert, but also gorgeous on its own, with a cup of tea for afternoon tea. In autumn, I love to serve it on a bed of warm quince syrup with a slice of poached quince (see page 175) and a little cream or ice cream. Or I swap the almond meal with hazelnut meal and add a little ground cinnamon. It's lovely with a little ground cardamom, too. It's definitely one to copy out, stick on the fridge and memorise for the repertoire.*

Because this cake seems to improve after a few hours (or even days if it's tightly wrapped), you can cook it a day ahead or early on the day you're serving it and then turn off the oven well before the kitchen starts to heat up.

SERVES 4–6
PREP TIME : 15 MINS ⟩ COOK TIME : 30 MINS

4 eggs, separated
1 cup (220 g) caster (superfine) sugar
1²/₃ cups (170 g) almond meal (see Note)
Finely grated zest of 1 orange
Icing (confectioners') sugar, for dusting
Fresh seasonal berries, to serve

Honey cream
¹/₄ cup (90 g) honey
1 cup (250 ml) thick (double) cream

Preheat the oven to 200°C (400°F). Grease a 20 cm (8 inch) square tin, a 20 cm (8 inch) spring-form tin or a 22 cm (8¹/₂ inch) ring tin. Line the tin with baking paper.

Use an electric mixer to beat the egg yolks and sugar together until thick and pale. Fold in the almond meal and orange zest.

Beat the egg whites in a separate bowl until stiff peaks form. Using a large metal spoon, gently fold the beaten egg white into the almond mixture. Pour the batter into the tin and bake for 30 minutes or until a skewer comes out clean. Cool in the tin for 5 minutes, then turn the cake out onto a wire rack to cool completely.

Just before serving, make the honey cream by stirring the honey through the cream.

Dust the cake with icing sugar and enjoy it with the honey cream and berries.

NOTE

I like to make my own almond meal by toasting whole natural almonds in a 180°C (350°F) oven for about 10 minutes, then blitzing the cooled nuts in my food processor to make a fine meal. This gives the cake a beautiful depth of flavour and flecked brown colour, but if you prefer the pure white of the almond meal from the shops, it's fine to use that.

A gentle dinner for a hot night

This menu is for those few weeks at the end of summer when the heat just does not give you a break, when you want to make and eat food to turn moods and people from frayed and frazzled to soothed and nourished. I'd suggest you try this on a late-summer evening, in the garden or the coolest part of your house; an easy, gentle procession of cool but bright and tasty food, finished off with one perfect scoop of ice cream.

We spent a gorgeous, golden evening over just such a menu in the village of Carcoar, New South Wales, in the home and garden of Belinda Satterthwaite. Belinda and her daughter Molly, their friends (also mother and daughter) Tanya and Ellie, my Alice and I had the loveliest time cooling off after a stinking hot January day. And the best part? Ice cream by the Belubula River for dessert.

This menu epitomises the kind of food I love to make and share – seasonal, simple and full of love and care. You could make a main meal of the rillettes and tomato salad if you liked. Or just serve the pasta. And if making your own ice cream sounds like a ridiculous thing to do, then just grab a tub of really nice store-bought stuff and maybe even drizzle it with a warm caramel sauce. Or not. Either way, I hope you enjoy these recipes – ideally in a garden somewhere, with friendly people and a nectarine shruboni in hand.

@tomolly_carcoar

NECTARINE SHRUB *(or shruboni)*
SALMON RILLETTES *with sliced baguette* ❦ TOMATO SALAD *with pesto*
FRESH RICOTTA *and* TOMATO PASTA *or*
CREAMED CORN PASTA *with chilli prosciutto crumbs*
SALTED CARAMEL ICE CREAM

*This menu epitomises the kind of food
I love to make and share.*

NECTARINE SHRUB

I feel like this is something that the Knights of Ni might like. Remember those indecisive fellows from Monty Python and the Holy Grail *who were after a shrubbery? Anyone with me? I do love making shrubs, which are basically a muddle of fruit, sugar and vinegar that, when you get the balance right, makes a very refreshing cordial or component to a more grown-up beverage like the shruboni below. Swap the nectarines for any stone fruit, or even berries, if you like.*

MAKES ABOUT 4 CUPS (1 LITRE)
PREP TIME : 15 MINS, PLUS CHILLING ꙮ COOK TIME : NIL

6 ripe, juicy nectarines, cut into chunks
2 cups (440 g) sugar
2 cups (500 ml) white balsamic vinegar
Chilled still or sparkling water, to serve

Put the nectarines and sugar in a large jar, screw on the lid and give the whole thing a good old shake. Pop the jar into the fridge for 24 hours, taking it out for a shake every now and then (twice in that time is enough).

The next day, strain out as much nectarine/sugar syrup as possible by pushing it through a fine mesh strainer. Pour this syrup into a clean glass bottle and add the balsamic vinegar. Seal with a lid and shake to combine. Leave the bottle in the fridge for at least 24 hours before using.

To serve, dilute the shrub with chilled still or sparkling water, to taste. I usually use about 30 ml (1 fl oz) shrub per 1 cup (250 ml) water, but taste as you go and adjust to suit.

Nectarine shruboni

Combine ¾ cup (185 ml) of the undiluted nectarine shrub with ¾ cup (185 ml) vermouth and ¾ cup (185 ml) gin in a jug. Cover and pop into the fridge until needed. Serve the nectarine shruboni over lots of ice or spritz it up into a punch by adding 1½ cups (375 ml) mineral water. Add two sliced nectarines and serve. *Makes about 4 cups (1 litre) to serve 4–6 people*

SALMON RILLETTES

I LOVE this recipe. It's gorgeous with fresh baguette as a starter as per this menu, alongside a rather delicious cocktail. It's also perfect for a summer lunch, served cold, in a big bowl with fresh or toasted baguette on the side. I have made it the star of just such a lunch, which also featured a supporting cast of crunchy chopped radishes, cucumber and cos lettuce salad, a platter of prosciutto-wrapped melon, some well-seasoned tomatoes tossed in olive oil and a mishmash of cheeses and cured meats. It was, I think, absolutely delicious – and a great way to feed a small or large group on a hot day. Plus, you can make the rillettes a day or two in advance and have it all ready to go when needed.

If there are any leftovers the next day (unlikely!), may I suggest you spread a tablespoon or two between two slices of soft white bread and slink off by yourself with a good book and a glass of chardonnay?

SERVES 4–6 AS A STARTER
PREP TIME : 20 MINS, PLUS CHILLING } COOK TIME : 10 MINS

2 cups (500 ml) white wine
2 French shallots, finely chopped
500 g (1 lb 2 oz) salmon fillets, cut into 1 cm (1/2 inch) pieces
1/2 cup (120 g) mayonnaise (page 102 or the best you can buy)
1/2 cup (125 g) crème fraîche
500 g (1 lb 2 oz) smoked salmon, roughly chopped
Juice of 1 lemon, or to taste
1/4 cup finely chopped dill
1 baguette, sliced, to serve

Start this recipe a day ahead. Put the wine and chopped shallots in a saucepan and bring to the boil. Reduce the heat to a simmer, add the salmon fillets and cook for a few minutes or until just translucent. Drain the salmon and shallots into a bowl, discarding the liquid. Cover and place in the fridge overnight or until completely cool.

Gently combine the poached salmon with the remaining ingredients. Season with salt and pepper to taste. You might find it needs a little more lemon, dill or even mayonnaise to suit your taste – keep tasting and tweaking until you're happy. Cover and return to the fridge until ready to serve with the sliced baguette.

TOMATO SALAD
with pesto

This salad is summer on a plate and would be a beautiful meal all on its own. Like all recipes with few ingredients, it relies on really good-quality ones. Ideally, use homegrown tomatoes, but otherwise buy some vine-ripened ones from the shops or market, along with a few lovely balls of fresh mozzarella. Make sure your tomatoes are at room temperature before you start – this does make a big difference to the flavour.

SERVES 4–6
PREP TIME : 10 MINS ❱ COOK TIME : NIL

700 g (1 lb 9 oz) mixed heirloom tomatoes
4 fresh mozzarella balls
1/4 cup (60 g) pesto (see Note)
2 Tbsp olive oil
Juice of 1 lemon
Chilli flakes, to serve

Thickly slice the tomatoes and arrange them on a serving platter. Tear the mozzarella balls into rough pieces and add them to the platter.

Spoon the pesto over the salad. Drizzle the olive oil and lemon juice over the top and season with freshly ground black pepper. Sprinkle the salad with chilli flakes, to taste.

NOTE
Use the recipe for nasturtium pesto from page 87, but use basil leaves instead of nasturtiums.

FRESH RICOTTA *and* TOMATO PASTA

One of my favourite pasta recipes of all! The only thing this sauce asks of you is a little time for the garlic to infuse the ricotta base, and some beautiful fresh tomatoes to bring it all to life. It's perfect fast food for high summer when boiling a pot of water is about as much cooking as you can handle.

SERVES 4
PREP TIME : 15 MINS ❱ COOK TIME : 15 MINS

1 large fresh mozzarella ball
1 cup (230 g) fresh ricotta cheese
3/4 cup (70 g) grated parmesan cheese
2 garlic cloves, finely chopped
2 cups (300 g) cherry tomatoes, halved
1 handful basil leaves
1/2 cup (125 ml) extra virgin olive oil
500 g (1 lb 2 oz) fettuccine

Shred the mozzarella ball into a large bowl and mix in the ricotta and parmesan. Add the garlic, cherry tomatoes, basil and olive oil. Stir until well combined, season well, then set aside at room temperature for 1 hour so all the flavours can get to know each other.

Cook the fettuccine in boiling salted water according to the packet instructions. Reserve 1/2 cup (125 ml) of the cooking water. Drain and tip the pasta straight into the bowl with the ricotta mixture. Gently stir to combine, adding some of the reserved cooking water to make the whole thing that much more slippery and delicious.

Transfer the pasta to a platter and serve immediately.

Store your tomatoes at room temperature for the best flavour.

CREAMED CORN PASTA
with chilli prosciutto crumbs

I think this pasta brings together everything we crave on a hot night when everyone arrives feeling itchy and tetchy – the comfort of carbs, the gentle, soft sweetness of fresh corn and the crunch and spice of the chilli prosciutto crumbs.

And can I just fly the flag here for proudly serving something so simple when friends come over for dinner? You might think you need to offer more, that a big beautiful bowl of pasta isn't fancy enough for company. But truly, simple is usually better, especially in this case. And especially when sandwiched between that beautiful starter of salmon rillettes and the salted caramel ice cream.

SERVES 4
PREP TIME : 20 MINS 〉 COOK TIME : 30 MINS

4 corn cobs
2 Tbsp (40 g) butter
2 spring onions (scallions), white part only, finely chopped
1 cup (250 ml) chicken or vegetable stock
2 Tbsp tarragon leaves
Juice of 1 lemon, or to taste
500 g (1 lb 2 oz) orecchiette pasta
100 g (3¹/₂ oz) crème fraîche
A few basil or other herb leaves, to serve

Chilli prosciutto crumbs
8 slices prosciutto
¹/₂ sourdough baguette or 4 slices sourdough bread, cut into cubes
¹/₄ cup (60 ml) olive oil
1 tsp chilli flakes, or to taste

For the crumbs, preheat the oven to 180°C (350°F) and place the prosciutto on a baking tray lined with baking paper. Place the bread cubes on another baking tray and drizzle with the olive oil. Bake for about 10 minutes or until the prosciutto is crispy and the bread is toasted and golden. Set aside until completely cool.

Blitz the prosciutto in a food processor until fine, then tip into a bowl. Blitz the sourdough cubes until fine, then mix with the prosciutto and chilli flakes.

Cut the corn kernels off the cobs. Melt the butter in a frying pan with a lid. Add the corn and spring onion and cook for about 5 minutes. Pour in the stock, add the tarragon and reduce the heat to low. Put the lid on and cook for 5 more minutes. Transfer the mixture to the food processor, reserving ¹/₄ cup (60 ml) of the corn mixture, and blend until smooth. Squeeze in the lemon juice to taste and season with sea salt and plenty of freshly ground black pepper. Return the purée to the pan with the reserved corn mixture and set aside.

Cook the pasta in boiling salted water according to the packet instructions. Reserve about 1 cup (250 ml) of the cooking water before draining the pasta.

Warm the creamed corn over low heat. Stir in the cooking water, a little at a time, until the sauce is silky. Add the drained pasta and crème fraîche and gently toss to combine.

Transfer the pasta to a serving platter, scatter generously with the chilli prosciutto crumbs and top with herbs. Serve immediately.

SALTED CARAMEL
ICE CREAM

Inspired by a recipe from the master David Lebovitz in his wonderful book, The Perfect Scoop, *this recipe takes his premise of making a caramel first, then adding milk and cream and whisking egg yolks and turning this into a custard. It's a recipe I have made countless times and it's always well received. Thank you, David!*

With an ice cream this rich, I think all you need is that one perfect scoop. If you have the time or inclination, it would also be wonderful alongside a few roasted plums or even roasted, sugared pineapple chunks. Yum.

MAKES ABOUT 4 CUPS (1 LITRE)
PREP TIME : 20 MINS, PLUS FREEZING ⁏ COOK TIME : 20 MINS

2 cups (500 ml) full-cream milk
1 cup (250 ml) single (pure) cream
1 vanilla bean, split lengthways
1 cup (220 g) caster (superfine) sugar
70 g (2^1/$_2$ oz) unsalted butter, cut into cubes
1 tsp salt
6 egg yolks

Combine the milk and cream in a saucepan. Scrape the vanilla seeds into the pan and add the scraped pod. Bring just to boiling point, then remove from the heat and set aside.

Tip the sugar into a large saucepan and place over medium–high heat. Melt the sugar into a dark golden caramel, swirling the pan around so the sugar melts evenly. Remove from the heat, add the butter and salt and whisk well until the butter melts. Don't worry if the mixture freaks out and seizes up a little (or a lot) – keep whisking and it should come together into a smooth caramel. Discard the vanilla pod from the warm milk mixture, then slowly pour it into the caramel, whisking to combine.

Whisk the egg yolks until well combined. Pour a little of the warm caramel milk into the egg yolks and whisk to combine, then gradually add the rest, whisking as you go. Tip the mixture back into the large saucepan. Cook over low heat, stirring constantly, for about 5 minutes or until the mixture thickens. Transfer to a jug and place in the fridge overnight.

Churn the chilled caramel mixture in an ice-cream machine.

Variation

Pour the thickened caramel mixture into a loaf tin lined with plastic wrap and freeze until firm, then turn it out and slice it as a semifreddo.

Ideas for the big family gathering

Whether it's for Christmas, a wedding, a wake, anniversary or important birthday, the 'big family gathering' is a big deal. And even the most functional of families can (and do) pull the odd drama out of their collective hat. So shouldn't food, or the feeding of big numbers, be the least of your worries? Here to help is my mum: Annie Herron, the master of feeding big groups with minimal fuss.

Every second year my parents host just over 30 of us at their farm for two days of Christmas. Yes, we all help, and we each contribute a dish or something, but really, the only reason it works is because of the planning and nothing-fazes-me (at least on the surface) attitude of my mother, aka 'the glue'.

None of this is to say that our family gatherings are perfect. But we all know that the good parts far, far outweigh any others. You know the magic that happens when cousins bunk in together and celebrate together, play together and put on plays together? When you get to really talk to your brother for the first time in months, albeit over a mountain of washing up? Or when you see your tween daughter having a deep and meaningful debrief (that you'll never know the details of) with your beautiful sister-in-law (she always gives the best advice)…

These moments make it all so worth the effort. And they are the ones you remember for a lovely long time, too.

Mum's tips on getting big groups together

- Fall back on family favourites and get everyone to contribute their own special dishes; repeat these every year because they are part of the memory and the ritual of these kinds of gatherings.
- Accept the fact that for weeks afterwards you'll be hunting for vegetable peelers or various dishes! When you have ten or twenty different people helping with washing up, nothing will be put back in the right place. But it will eventually find its way back home.

@artclasseswithannieherron

RICE PUDDING ❯ *Mum's* STEAMED WHOLE SALMON *with lots of herbs*
Roasted CHERRY TOMATO, SALMON *and* YOGHURT SALAD
Salt-and-vinegar HASSELBACK POTATOES
CHICKEN POTATO SALAD *with salsa verde*
ELDERFLOWER *and* PROSECCO JELLIES *with cream and berries*

The special moments that make the big family gathering so worth the effort are the ones you remember for a lovely long time.

RICE PUDDING

*This would have to be my favourite recipe in the whole book. Apart from its deliciousness, it's because of the role it plays in our family playbook of rituals. Inspired by my Danish grandfather's own family traditions, every Christmas Eve we commence the meal with a small bowl of rice pudding (*risengrød*) topped with a cube of butter and a good sprinkle of cinnamon sugar. A blanched almond is hidden in one of the bowls and the person who finds it must hide that fact until the end of the meal. If they succeed in keeping it hidden, they get a little gift – usually a box of choccies.*

The excitement over who would get the almond every year always ran high when we were kids and now I see my kids and their cousins enjoying the whole game just as much. Rice pudding also happens to be one of my kids' favourite comfort foods. They especially love it cold for lunches. Me too.

SERVES 8
PREP TIME : 5 MINS ⟩ COOK TIME : 45 MINS

2 cups (400 g) arborio rice
8 cups (2 litres) full-cream milk
1/2 cup (110 g) caster (superfine) sugar
1 vanilla bean, split lengthways
Cold, cubed butter, to serve

Cinnamon sugar
1/2 cup (110 g) caster (superfine) sugar
1/4 tsp ground cinnamon, or to taste

Put the rice in a large saucepan and add 3/4 cup (185 ml) water. Bring to the boil, stirring often so the rice doesn't catch on the bottom of the pan, then cook for 2 minutes. Add the milk and sugar, scrape in the vanilla seeds and add the pod. Stir well and cook over low heat, stirring occasionally, for 35–40 minutes or until the rice is cooked through.

For the cinnamon sugar, mix together the sugar and cinnamon (add some more cinnamon if you like it stronger).

Remove the rice from the heat and serve warm with a knob of butter and a sprinkling of cinnamon sugar.

NOTE
The rice pudding is also lovely served cold with poached fruit or a dollop of the apricot purée from page 19. You'll find that it firms up on cooling – I generally add 1 cup (250 ml) of milk (or cream if I'm feeling indulgent) to loosen it up before reheating or serving chilled.

Mum's STEAMED WHOLE SALMON
with lots of herbs

This is what we have pretty much every time there's a big family gathering. The fish steams on the stovetop in under an hour, so there's no carry on with hot ovens, shoving your head into the oven to baste or check or worry if that massive turkey or whatever is cooked. Plus, it's cool and fresh and delicious. And a whole salmon, while not cheap, does go a long way and makes feeding a big group so easy, with leftovers as well. I recommend you order the salmon from your fishmonger in advance, and ask them to gut and scale the fish for you.

You do need to invest in a fish kettle – a long, skinny rectangular saucepan with a rack inside. Mum bought one years ago and it does the rounds of the family all year. You could make do with a large roasting tin with a wire rack placed in the middle – it just needs to be able to go over a hotplate or gas ring.

SERVES 8–10
PREP TIME : 15 MINS ❧ COOK TIME : 50 MINS

1 large whole salmon, about 3 kg (6 lb 12 oz)
2 brown onions, thinly sliced
2 handfuls parsley
1 handful dill
2 lemons, thinly sliced, plus extra lemon
   slices to serve
1 handful mixed herbs (I like a mix of dill,
   mint and parsley), to serve
1 large telegraph cucumber, sliced, to serve

Dill sauce
1 cup (300 g) mayonnaise (page 102
   or the best you can buy)
1/4 cup (85 g) sour cream
Juice of 2 lemons
1 handful dill, finely chopped

For the dill sauce, combine all the ingredients in a jug and mix to make a fairly runny sauce. Taste and adjust the seasoning. Pop the sauce into the fridge until needed.

Rinse the salmon and pat dry. Stuff the cavity with the onion, herbs and lemon slices. Sprinkle in plenty of sea salt and cracked black pepper. Place the fish on the rack inside a fish kettle or large roasting tin. Add about 2 cm (3/4 inch) cold water or enough to just reach the bottom of the fish (you don't want the water to entirely cover the fish – we're steaming here, not poaching). Place the lid on top of the fish kettle or cover the roasting tin with foil.

Place the kettle or roasting tin over the biggest hotplate or gas ring. Bring the water to the boil and cook for 5 minutes, then turn off the heat and stand for 30–45 minutes, depending on how cooked you like your fish – we like our salmon nice and pink in the centre. Don't be tempted to uncover the fish while it's steaming – leave it for 30 minutes before checking it.

To serve, peel back the salmon skin and remove the tail and head. Place the fish on a platter and arrange the extra lemon slices on top. Surround the fish with cucumber and fresh herbs. Get the best carver in the family to do the honours, ensuring all bones are removed.

Serve the salmon with the dill sauce and a crunchy salad, such as the slaw from page 14.

Recipe pictured page 125, top left

Roasted CHERRY TOMATO, SALMON and YOGHURT SALAD

This is my take on that fabulous and famous Ottolenghi recipe where he piles roasted cherry tomatoes on cold yoghurt. Here we are adding left-over salmon and nigella seeds and, when served with a crunchy baguette and maybe some rocket (arugula) on the side, it becomes a beautiful summer lunch that I'd happily eat every day. In place of steamed salmon, you could use hot-smoked salmon or trout, or even poached chicken.

SERVES 8
PREP TIME : 20 MINS } COOK TIME : 20 MINS

700 g (1 lb 9 oz) cherry tomatoes
1/3 cup (80 ml) olive oil
Grated zest and juice of 3 limes
1 cup (260 g) thick, full-fat Greek-style yoghurt
700 g (1 lb 9 oz) left-over steamed salmon, broken into chunks
1/4 cup (40 g) nigella seeds

Preheat the oven to 200°C (400°F). Place the cherry tomatoes in a roasting tin, drizzle with the olive oil and sprinkle with the lime zest. Sprinkle with some sea salt and freshly ground black pepper.

Roast for 20 minutes or until the tomatoes are collapsed and beginning to char on top (but no longer or they'll turn to mush and won't look as pretty).

Meanwhile, spread the yoghurt over the base of a serving bowl or platter. Top with the hot cherry tomatoes, then the salmon chunks. Sprinkle with the nigella seeds, squeeze the lime juice over the top and serve.

This salad is a beautiful way to use any left-over steamed salmon.

Recipe pictured page 125, top right

Salt-and-vinegar
HASSELBACK POTATOES

These look gorgeous, taste fabulous and are, I think, the perfect accompaniment to the steamed salmon with dill sauce on this festive table... but they would be beautiful at any table, on any occasion.

SERVES 8
PREP TIME : 15 MINS, PLUS OVERNIGHT DRYING ⟩ COOK TIME : 1 HOUR

3 kg (6 lb 12 oz) roasting potatoes
1/4 cup (60 ml) olive oil
2 tsp thyme leaves

Salt-and-vinegar seasoning
1/4 cup (35 g) sea salt flakes
1/3 cup (80 ml) malt vinegar
1 tsp cornflour (cornstarch)

To make the seasoning, combine the sea salt, vinegar and cornflour in a bowl and mix well. Spread the mixture over a baking tray and leave it to dry out at room temperature overnight. It will harden, so use a pestle or fork to break it up into a salty consistency. You can store the seasoning in a jar for a month or so.

Preheat the oven to 200°C (400°F). Place a potato on your chopping board and carefully make evenly spaced cuts, about 5 mm (1/4 inch) apart, three-quarters of the way through the potato. Place the potato in a large bowl and repeat with the remaining potatoes.

Drizzle the olive oil over the potatoes and sprinkle with the thyme, then toss so that the potatoes are well covered with oil.

Arrange the potatoes in a roasting tin and bake for 1 hour or until they are really, really crunchy and golden. Keep cooking if you feel they aren't quite there yet – that golden crunch is really the key to these spuds. As soon as you take the potatoes out of the oven, sprinkle them with about 2 tablespoons of the salt-and-vinegar seasoning (or to taste). Serve hot.

Recipe pictured page 125, bottom left

CHICKEN POTATO SALAD
with salsa verde

This is another fabulous cold lunch option that will happily make the most of left-over Christmas turkey or chicken. But don't just save it for that – poach a couple of chicken breasts or buy a roast chook from the shops and shred it for this dish. It's a great one to take to work for lunch and also makes a really nice main meal if you're having friends over and it's too hot to cook.

SERVES 8
PREP TIME : 20 MINS ⟩ COOK TIME : 15 MINS

700 g (1 lb 9 oz) left-over cooked chicken or turkey (roasted,
    poached, barbecued – whatever!)
1 kg (2 lb 4 oz) baby potatoes
1 cup (250 ml) Salsa verde (page 15)
3 cups (135 g) mixed rocket (arugula) and baby spinach
1/2 cup (50 g) flaked almonds, toasted
A few mint leaves

Shred the cooked chicken or turkey.

Steam or boil the potatoes until completely tender when pierced with a knife. Set aside to cool a little.

Toss the warm potatoes with the chicken, salsa verde, rocket and spinach, almonds and mint leaves.

Variation

If you have any dill sauce left over from the salmon, absolutely use this instead of the salsa verde – it will be just as delicious.

Recipe pictured page 125, bottom right

ELDERFLOWER *and* PROSECCO JELLIES
with cream and berries

I think jellies are one of the very best ways to end a meal. They're light and cleansing and just the right amount of sweetness, and you can always fit a little glass of jelly in despite feeling completely full. And, like many of the desserts in this book, they are all done and ready to pass around well before anyone arrives. Obviously this is one for the adults, but if you prefer you can leave out the prosecco, increase the cordial by 1/2 cup (125 ml) and make up the rest of the liquid with water.

I especially love elderflower jellies, but this recipe would work well with any fruit syrup or cordial you have on hand.

SERVES 8
PREP TIME : 10 MINS, PLUS SETTING ⚘ COOK TIME : 5 MINS

4 gold-strength gelatine leaves (see Note)
1¹/2 cups (375 ml) undiluted elderflower cordial
2 cups (500 ml) prosecco or sparkling wine
Fresh raspberries, to serve
Whipped cream, to serve

Put the gelatine leaves in a shallow bowl and pour in 1 cup (250 ml) cold water. Set aside to soften.

Meanwhile, combine the elderflower cordial and 1 cup (250 ml) water in a small saucepan and bring to the boil. Remove from the heat.

Squeeze the liquid out of the gelatine leaves and add them to the pan. Whisk until the gelatine has completely dissolved. Pour in the prosecco and gently stir.

Divide the mixture among pretty serving glasses, add a small handful of raspberries to each glass and pop the jellies into the fridge to set for at least 3 hours.

Serve the jellies topped with a dollop of whipped cream.

NOTE

Check the gelatine packet to see how much you need – most will tell you how many sheets you need to set every 1 cup (250 ml) of liquid.

AUTUMN

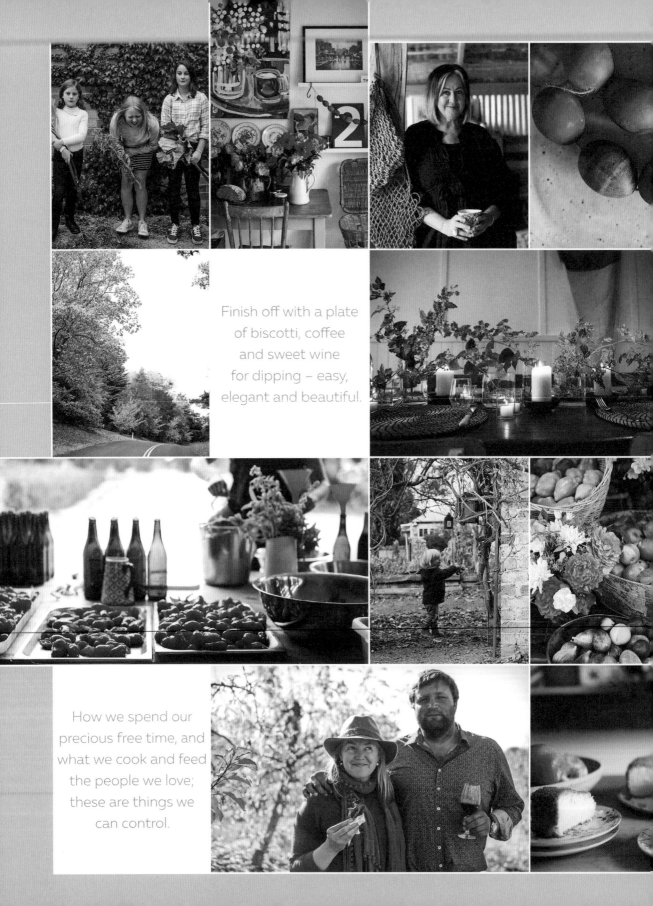

Finish off with a plate
of biscotti, coffee
and sweet wine
for dipping – easy,
elegant and beautiful.

How we spend our
precious free time, and
what we cook and feed
the people we love;
these are things we
can control.

Stave off the Sunday night blues and end the weekend on a high with an early supper followed by cards or charades.

Conviviality is our superpower - bringing people together to share a meal is an important act.

Beating the Sunday night blues

I spent my last few years of school as a boarder and, while I loved the experience, the 'Sunday blues' did creep up on me around 2pm every weekend home. I still get a funny feeling in my tummy on Sunday afternoons – that memory of packing up after a weekend of home comforts, heading to the train station and saying goodbye to Mum and Dad for another few weeks.

If you get the Sunday blues, like many of us do, here's a little trick to stave them off: organise an activity to stretch your weekend out that bit longer. Meet a couple of families at the park, go for a bushwalk, see a movie or, best of all, have a games evening. Throw something easy in the oven, set the table nicely and enjoy a meal together, followed by a round or two of your favourite board game or card game. Share some laughs, then send everyone home with plenty of time to get sorted for the week ahead.

Few families love a games night as much as Emma, Gep, Charlie and Sophia Blake. I was at school with Em and know that she shares my love of a Sunday afternoon gathering. She's also a super-talented florist and has shared some tips on how to make the table look a bit special without spending a cent.

Emma's tips for making your table beautiful

Look for one gorgeous growing thing – something that's healthy and vibrant; interesting in shape, movement and texture; possibly fragrant or colourful, delicate or bold. Let the natural form be the guide to how you shape and work it onto your table – straight lines, cluster and repetition, tendrils and vines climbing over each other – let it flow and interact with the place settings. I also love using single stems and playing with varying heights. Here I've used porcelain vine from our garden fence and lots of candles. Other homegrown or foraged foliage or florals that can be used in a similar way include honeysuckle, rosemary, hawthorn, ivy, native grasses, Queen Anne's lace, eucalyptus, privet berry, salvia, succulents, wild fennel, mint, climbing roses, ferns or fruit blossoms.

@emmablakefloral

BAKED PASTA *with* FENNEL SAUSAGE

CRUNCHY SALAD *(page 79)* ❧ GARLIC BREAD

ROLLED PAVLOVA *with* HAZELNUT PRALINE
and Sophia's RHUBARB COMPOTE

Finishing your weekend on a high makes the week ahead seem that much more exciting.

BAKED PASTA *with* FENNEL SAUSAGE

This crowd-pleasing comfort food is a simple concoction of pasta in a rich tomato and fennel sausage ragu, topped with a layer of nutmeg-spiced bechamel and some breadcrumbs for crunch. Make it in advance so that when Sunday afternoon arrives, the kitchen is tidy, dinner is bubbling away in the oven and everyone's happy. And ideally, make a double batch and stash one in the freezer or drop it off to a friend needing sustenance and love.

SERVES 6

PREP TIME : 30 MINS   COOK TIME : 3 HOURS

1/3 cup (80 ml) olive oil

1 kg (2 lb 4 oz) thick Italian sausages with fennel (or your favourite fancy sausages)

2 brown onions, diced

6 garlic cloves, finely chopped

2 Tbsp thyme leaves, finely chopped

2 Tbsp rosemary leaves, finely chopped

2 cups (500 ml) tomato passata (puréed tomatoes)

800 g (1 lb 12 oz) tin whole peeled Italian tomatoes (or the same amount of fresh tomatoes, roughly chopped)

500 g (1 lb 2 oz) orecchiette or penne pasta

2 cups (140 g) sourdough breadcrumbs

1/2 cup (45 g) grated parmesan cheese

Bechamel sauce

100 g (3 1/2 oz) butter

1/2 cup (75 g) plain (all-purpose) flour

5 cups (1.25 litres) full-cream milk, warmed

1/2 tsp freshly grated nutmeg

1 cup (95 g) grated parmesan cheese

Heat the olive oil in a large heavy-based saucepan over medium–high heat. Squeeze the sausage meat out of the casings and into the pan. Brown the meat, stirring and breaking it up as it cooks, for about 5 minutes. Add the onion and cook for about 5 minutes, stirring often. Add the garlic and herbs and cook for 5 minutes or until the onion is completely cooked through and lovely and soft. Add the passata and tinned or fresh tomatoes and give it all a good stir. Reduce the heat to low and cook, stirring often, for 2 hours.

Meanwhile, for the bechamel sauce, melt the butter in a saucepan. Just as it is starting to froth and inch towards turning brown, add the flour and whisk for a minute or so until the butter and flour come together into a sandy paste. Add 1/2 cup (125 ml) of the milk and whisk quickly until you have a smooth paste, then add the rest of the milk, 1/2 cup at a time, whisking after each addition, and cook until you have a beautiful, thick white sauce. Remove from the heat and add the nutmeg, parmesan and some salt and pepper, stirring until combined and smooth.

Preheat the oven to 200°C (400°F). Cook the pasta in boiling salted water according to the packet instructions. Reserve 1 cup (250 ml) of the cooking water before draining the pasta. Stir the pasta through the ragu, adding the reserved water if it needs a little more moisture. Tip the ragu into a large ovenproof serving dish, pour the bechamel sauce over the top and sprinkle it with the sourdough breadcrumbs and grated parmesan.

Pop the dish into the oven for 40 minutes or so until the top is golden and the bechamel sauce is bubbling through the breadcrumbs.

Garlic bread

Nobody loves garlic bread as much as my girl Alice. Except perhaps every teenager I've ever met.

Preheat the oven to 200°C (400°F). Finely chop 1 small handful of parsley and 5 fat garlic cloves. Combine the parsley and garlic with the grated zest of 1 lemon, ½ cup (45 g) grated parmesan cheese and 120 g (4¼ oz) softened butter. Season to taste.

Cut a baguette into 2.5 cm (1 inch) slices, being careful not to slice all the way through. Spread each slice with a little of the garlic butter, then spread a little more across the top of the baguette. Wrap the baguette in foil and bake for 25 minutes. Cut the foil open to expose the top of the baguette and return it to the oven for a final 10 minutes to crisp it up.

Sophia's
RHUBARB COMPOTE

*Serve this compote with pretty much anything.
It's lovely over porridge with a splash of milk,
swirled through yoghurt with granola in summer,
in a crumble, over ice cream or, best of all, next
to the beautiful pavlova roulade. Thank you to
Sophia Blake (aged 10) for this recipe.*

MAKES ABOUT 2 CUPS
PREP TIME : 10 MINS ⟩ COOK TIME : 15 MINS

1 bunch (about 300 g/10^{1}/$_{2}$ oz) trimmed rhubarb,
    cut into small pieces
^{3}/$_{4}$ cup (165 g) sugar, or to taste
Grated zest and juice of 1 orange
1 vanilla bean, split lengthways

Combine the rhubarb, sugar, orange zest and juice
in a saucepan with ^{1}/$_{4}$ cup (60 ml) water. Scrape the
vanilla seeds into the pan and add the scraped pod.

Cook over medium–low heat for 15 minutes or until
the rhubarb has broken down and is completely soft
and delicious. Taste and stir in a little more sugar
(or some honey) if needed.

Pudding 'hall pass'

If you run out of puff when it comes to making
pudding, just give yourself a break and fill a few
little bowls with chocolate honeycomb, Maltesers
or other yummy sweets to pass around while
you're playing games. There'll be no complaints,
I promise!

ROLLED PAVLOVA
with HAZELNUT PRALINE

This pudding ticks every box for me. Most importantly, it's made well in advance and then just sits there, all rolled and cute in the fridge, ready to be gobbled up. Secondly, it's a light ending to a heavier main and, thanks to the rhubarb, not too sweet.

Don't be at all put off about the whole 'rolling the pav' element – truly, it's easy and because you cover the top with cream and praline, any cracks or mistakes are easily hidden.

SERVES 6
PREP TIME : 15 MINS, PLUS CHILLING ❦ COOK TIME : 20 MINS

4 egg whites
1 cup (220 g) caster (superfine) sugar
2 Tbsp cornflour (cornstarch)
1 tsp white vinegar
1 tsp vanilla bean paste
1 quantity Hazelnut praline (page 80)
2 cups (500 ml) single (pure) cream
Rhubarb compote, to serve (see left)

Preheat the oven to 150°C (300°F). Line a 26 x 38 cm (10½ x 15 inch) Swiss roll tin with baking paper.

Place the egg whites in the bowl of an electric mixer fitted with the whisk attachment. Whisk until soft peaks form. Add all but 2 tablespoons of the sugar, a little at a time, then beat for a further 5 minutes. Sift in half of the cornflour, add the vinegar and vanilla and gently fold to combine.

Spoon the mixture into the tin and smooth the top so it's nice and even, then pop it into the oven for 20 minutes or until just firm. Remove the pavlova from the oven and set it aside to cool for 5 minutes.

While the pavlova is cooking, make the praline according to the recipe.

Combine the remaining sugar and cornflour in a small bowl. Place a sheet of baking paper on your work surface and dust it with the sugar mixture. Gently turn the pavlova out onto the dusted baking paper, then peel off the baking paper from the base. Leave the pavlova to cool completely.

Whip the cream until thick and soft. Spread the cream along one long edge of the pavlova, reserving a little for the top. Carefully roll the pavlova over the cream into a log shape, then spread the remaining cream over the top. Gently transfer the pavlova to a serving plate and pop it into the fridge for at least an hour.

Before serving, trim the edges of the pavlova roll. Sprinkle the hazelnut praline over the top and serve with the warm rhubarb compote.

Passata day at Girragirra

At the time of writing we are in lockdown, waiting for the Covid-19 crisis to pass. I keep coming back to this quote shared on Instagram by one of my favourite food writers, Carla Lalli Music: 'I know there's a lot to be unsure of right now, but for those of us who love to cook, there's a lot to feel positive about, too. You can continue to feed yourself, your family – and others, if that feels safe – and I hope that in doing so, you find relief, and a release.'

There is so much we can't control in life. So much in the news that makes us sad or scared or bewildered. But how we come together, how we spend our Sundays and what we cook and feed the people we love... these things we can control. I'm not talking about fancy, expensive food and gatherings, but simple, tasty food that's real and good and full of love. I think that conviviality is our secret superpower – that bringing people together to share a meal is an important act that can change outlooks, brighten moods and make us feel connected in a very powerful way.

Kim and Wendy Muffet of Girragirra Retreat in Forbes, New South Wales, are all about conviviality and also happen to be the growers and makers of some of the tastiest food I've ever enjoyed. It was a pleasure to make lunch for their family in the midst of their annual 'passata day'. As it happens, this shoot was the last outing I had for some months. We began socially isolating just days afterwards, so that sunny Saturday lunch under the grapevines in Forbes holds a special place in my memory.

Wendy's tips for making things easy when friends come over

I would love to be one of those people who has everything done an hour before guests arrive – cool, calm and collected, glass in hand. But to be honest, all is well if I manage to have the table set with something lovely from the garden (flowers, fruit, pretty weeds!) and some upbeat music on. I also try to have the pre-dinner snacks and drinks ready to go. We like to keep these simple and tasty and look to the garden for inspiration – one big platter laden with local olives, a pickle and house-made hummus with crisp veggies from the garden and various kinds of sourdough bits is a favourite.

@girragirra

LITTLE HERB PIES *with pickles*
POLPETTONE *in tomato sauce with greens and sourdough*
WENDY'S CURTIDO
WALNUT *and* FENNEL BISCOTTI *with sweet wine and fresh figs*

Bringing people together to share a meal can change outlooks, brighten moods and make us feel connected.

LITTLE HERB PIES *with pickles*

These little pies are heaven as a starter or, when made a little larger, as a main meal, perhaps with bread and butter pickles and the Crunchy salad from page 79. You could also make one beautiful galette by rolling the pastry into a big round and piling the herby filling and some tomatoes on top before baking. Either way, I hope you love this recipe as much as I do.

A quick note on the pastry, which is inspired by the wonderful Maggie Beer: this recipe makes a short, flaky pastry that's just perfect here, but if you have sheets of shortcrust or puff in the freezer, those would be great, too. Also, I find it easiest to make the filling mixture in advance and have it chilled when it comes to assembling your pies.

SERVES 6–8

PREP TIME : 25 MINS, PLUS 50 MINUTES CHILLING ❧ COOK TIME : 30 MINS

1 Tbsp olive oil
2 brown onions, thinly sliced
1/2 cup (125 g) sour cream
110 g (3¾ oz) goat's cheese, crumbled
1 handful mixed herbs (see Note)
2 eggs
2 Tbsp single (pure) cream
Sesame seeds, for sprinkling
Sea salt flakes, for sprinkling
Pickle or tomato relish, to serve

Sour cream pastry
²/3 cup (160 g) sour cream
1 cup (250 g) chilled unsalted butter,
   cut into cubes
2 cups (300 g) plain (all-purpose) flour,
   plus extra for dusting
1/2 tsp sea salt

Heat the olive oil in a large frying pan over medium heat. Cook the onion for 10 minutes or until completely softened and caramelised. Transfer the onion to a bowl to cool.

Meanwhile, make the pastry. Put the sour cream, butter, flour and salt in a food processor and blitz for a few seconds until just combined. Turn the pastry out onto a work surface and gently bring it together into a disc. Wrap the pastry and pop it into the fridge for 30 minutes.

Add the sour cream, goat's cheese, herbs and 1 egg to the onion and gently mix to combine.

Roll out the pastry on a lightly floured surface until 3 mm (⅛ inch) thick. Using a biscuit cutter or glass, cut the pastry into 7 cm (2¾ inch) rounds. Place about a tablespoon of the herb mixture in the middle of a pastry round and bring the sides together, pressing to seal. Use the tines of a fork to gently press down around the edges. Place the pie on a baking tray lined with baking paper. Repeat with the remaining pastry and filling. Place the pies in the fridge for about 20 minutes. Preheat the oven to 200°C (400°F).

Whisk the remaining egg with the cream, then brush it over the pies and sprinkle them with the sesame seeds and sea salt flakes. Bake for 20 minutes or until the pies are golden and the pastry has puffed up. Serve the warm pies with a tangy pickle or tomato relish.

NOTE

My favourite mix of herbs for these pies is parsley, mint, sorrel and tarragon. Try to avoid woody herbs like thyme and rosemary as they might overpower the mixture.

POLPETTONE *in tomato sauce*

This prosciutto-wrapped terrine baked in a puddle of tasty tomato sauce and sprinkled with parmesan is a total winner – that perfect marriage of the familiar with a few twists. It sits firmly in the comfort food column, but is fancy enough to serve when friends come over. Serve it with crusty bread and mixed lettuce dressed with olive oil and lemon juice.

Because there was a wood-fired oven lit and ready to go, we finished off the dish in there, but a regular hot oven is fine.

SERVES 8
PREP TIME : 25 MINS, PLUS OVERNIGHT CHILLING 〉 COOK TIME : 2³/4 HOURS

2 cups (120 g) fresh breadcrumbs
¹/2 cup (125 ml) milk
2 Tbsp olive oil
1 onion, diced
3 garlic cloves, finely chopped
500 g (1 lb 2 oz) pork mince
500 g (1 lb 2 oz) beef mince
2 eggs
2 tsp dijon mustard
1 large handful sage leaves, finely chopped
1 Tbsp rosemary leaves, finely chopped
2 Tbsp parsley leaves, finely chopped

¹/4 tsp freshly grated nutmeg
8 slices prosciutto
1 cup (95 g) grated parmesan cheese

Tomato sauce
¹/4 cup (60 ml) olive oil
1 brown onion, finely chopped
2 garlic cloves, finely chopped
800 g (1 lb 12 oz) tin whole peeled Italian tomatoes
6 basil leaves
¹/4 cup (60 ml) red wine vinegar
1 tsp sugar

Preheat the oven to 180°C (350°F). Combine the breadcrumbs and milk in a small bowl and leave to soften.

Heat the olive oil in a frying pan over medium heat. Cook the onion for 10 minutes. Add the garlic and cook for 2 minutes, stirring often. Leave to cool, then tip the mixture into a large bowl. Add the breadcrumb mixture, along with the pork, beef, eggs, mustard, herbs, nutmeg and about a teaspoon each of salt and freshly ground black pepper.

Line a 30 x 12 cm (12 x 4¹/2 inch) loaf tin with the prosciutto, leaving the slices overhanging the sides. Firmly pack the meat mixture into the tin. Fold the prosciutto over the top and tightly cover with foil. Place in a roasting tin and carefully pour in boiling water to come halfway up the sides of the loaf tin. Bake for 1 hour or until the meatloaf is cooked through.

Remove the loaf tin from the water and weigh the meatloaf down with a few tins of tomatoes (or whatever is in the pantry), then pop it into the fridge to cool completely, preferably overnight.

For the sauce, heat the olive oil in a large heavy-based frying pan over medium heat. Cook the onion for 10 minutes or until soft and just beginning to caramelise. Add the garlic and cook for 2 minutes. Tip in the tomatoes and break them up with a spoon. Cook over low heat for 30 minutes, stirring often. Add the basil, vinegar and sugar and cook for 20 minutes.

About 40 minutes before you're ready to eat, preheat the oven to 200°C (400°F). Turn the meatloaf out into a roasting tin or ovenproof serving platter with high sides. Pour the tomato sauce over the meatloaf, sprinkle the parmesan over the top and cook for 30 minutes or until the meatloaf is completely heated through and the cheese is melted and golden.

WENDY'S CURTIDO

This is Wendy's recipe for curtido, a kind of Salvadorian sauerkraut. It's bright pink and so, so delicious with any rich food or just with a fried egg and some rice and greens. I love the sweetness that comes from the fresh pineapple and it was just perfect with the polpettone.

MAKES TWO 4 CUP (1 LITRE) JARS
PREP TIME : 20 MINS, PLUS 5–10 DAYS FERMENTING ⟩ COOK TIME : NIL

1.5 kg (3 lb 5 oz) purple cabbage
600 g (1 lb 5 oz) green cabbage
300 g (10$^{1}/_{2}$ oz) carrots, grated
1 white onion, thinly sliced
1 Tbsp salt
1 cup (160 g) fresh pineapple chunks
    (optional, but delicious!)
2 chillies (traditionally jalapeños),
    roughly chopped
3–5 cm (1$^{1}/_{4}$–2 inch) piece fresh ginger,
    grated
3 oregano sprigs, leaves picked

Remove and wash the outer cabbage leaves. Set aside. Slice the remaining cabbage as finely as you can, discarding the hard cores. Combine the cabbage, carrot and onion in a large bowl.

Sprinkle the vegetables with the salt, then massage the mixture until it drips like a wet sponge when you squeeze a handful. Add the pineapple (if using), chilli, ginger and oregano. Use your hands to mix well.

Pack the mixture into two 4 cup (1 litre) jars, pushing down after each handful to remove any air pockets and force the liquid to rise. Leave 4 cm (1$^{1}/_{2}$ inches) free at the top of the jars. Check that the vegetable mixture is covered by the juices. If not, make up a brine by dissolving 3 teaspoons salt in 4 cups (1 litre) water and use it to cover the vegetables.

Cover the vegetables with a reserved cabbage leaf and hold it in place with some kind of plug (e.g. a carrot cut to size or a small shot glass). The goal is to keep all of the mixture under the brine and away from air so it doesn't go mouldy.

Secure the lid and leave the mixture to ferment on the bench, out of direct sunlight, for 5–10 days (the time will depend on the temperature of the room – the warmer it is, the faster it will ferment). Taste the mixture after 5 days. When it's ready, it will be crunchy and tangy. Taste it every few days until it's ready, but pop it into the fridge before it gets too sour.

WALNUT *and* FENNEL BISCOTTI

Biscotti are such a handy thing to bake. They last for weeks in an airtight container, are easy to make and, when served with some fresh fruit and sweet wine or coffee to dip into, they are a lovely elegant way to end a meal. Plus, there's no mess, no plating up and no more washing up.

MAKES 20
PREP TIME : 20 MINS, PLUS CHILLING ⁂ COOK TIME : 40 MINS

1 cup (115 g) walnuts
1 tsp fennel seeds
1¼ cups (185 g) plain (all-purpose) flour
¼ cup (50 g) polenta
1 tsp ground cinnamon
½ tsp baking powder
A pinch of salt
75 g (2½ oz) unsalted butter, softened
⅔ cup (150 g) caster (superfine) sugar
1 egg
1 tsp vanilla extract
Grated zest of 1 orange

Preheat the oven to 180°C (350°F). Line two baking trays with baking paper.

Spread the walnuts and fennel seeds on a baking tray and bake for 10 minutes or until fragrant and just toasted. Transfer to a mortar and pestle and roughly pound (or roughly chop them using a large sharp knife). Set aside to cool.

In a small bowl, whisk together the flour, polenta, cinnamon, baking powder and salt.

Using an electric mixer, cream the butter and sugar until light and fluffy. Add the egg, vanilla and orange zest and beat until well combined. Add the flour mixture and beat until just combined. Fold in the walnut and fennel seed mixture. Wrap the dough and place it in the fridge to rest for 20 minutes.

Divide the dough in half and shape each piece into a log about 4 cm (1½ inches) wide. Place each log on a baking tray and bake for 20 minutes. Set aside to cool.

Using a serrated knife, cut the logs into slices about 2 cm (¾ inch) thick. Arrange in a single layer on the trays and return to the oven for 10 minutes.

Allow the biscotti to cool completely on a wire rack and then store them in an airtight container for up to 2 weeks. Serve with sweet wine or coffee for dipping.

The visitor cake

When I moved to the country some 15 years ago, my mum advised me to master a basic cake recipe so that whenever visitors came over there was something freshly baked at the ready. That's a bit extreme, I thought. What's wrong with a packet of biscuits? The answer, of course, is nothing at all. But, with a little hindsight and many cakes later, I agree with Mum. It is always so appreciated when you have something home-made to greet your visitors.

And just as it's lovely to have a warm cake or scone at the ready for unexpected guests, it's also pretty lovely to rock up to a friend's place with a basket of warm scones and something like the hummingbird loaf that we took to visit Tania Robinson of Southern Wild Co. We joined Tania and her partner Matt for morning tea at their extraordinary woolshed in country New South Wales on a freezing May morning. I took Mum and my daughter and we spent the loveliest few hours talking about art, playing with their beautiful puppy and just enjoying the space and company.

Tania's ideas for setting the scene when friends visit

Nothing gives us more pleasure than to gather around our big wooden table in the Southern Wild Co 'shedquarters' with friends and family to share home-cooked food. I love to have one of our candles burning and choose a complementary scent that won't clash with the food. Candlelight elevates the mood with a warm, cosy glow and makes your gathering extra special. I always have a small bouquet of fragrant herbs, flowers or even some succulents, freshly picked from the garden, on the table in one of our repurposed bush poetry glasses. Mismatched tableware, often cherished items handed down from my grandmother, or rustic local pottery completes the scene and creates a relaxed and inviting setting.

@southernwildco

The 'ORIGINAL' VISITOR CAKE
RHUBARB, ORANGE *and* PISTACHIO THUMBPRINTS
PEAR, WALNUT *and* NUTMEG CAKE
HUMMINGBIRD LOAF CAKE ❧ CINNAMON *and* FRUIT SCONES
FIG *and* ALMOND CAKE *that thinks it's a tart*

It is always so appreciated when you have something home-made to greet your visitors.

The 'ORIGINAL' VISITOR CAKE

This is one of the most useful 'basic' recipes I can think of. Pretty much bomb-proof, it's based on the traditional French butter cake 'quartre-quart' recipe so the quantities are easy to remember and the method is très simple. Plus it's delicious and, as per my notes below, you can take this one in lots of different, seasonal directions so it's a great basic cake recipe to have up your sleeve. If you need a chocolate birthday cake, just add some cocoa, or if you'd like a fruit slice, spoon the batter into a high-sided roasting tin and dot the top with fresh fruit. And so on.

SERVES 6-8
PREP TIME : 15 MINS COOK TIME : 35 MINS

1 cup (250 g) butter, softened
250 g (9 oz) caster (superfine) sugar
1 tsp vanilla bean paste
4 eggs
$1^2/_3$ cups (250 g) self-raising flour

Preheat the oven to 180°C (350°F). Grease a 20 cm (8 inch) spring-form tin.

Combine the butter and sugar in the bowl of an electric mixer and beat until pale and fluffy. Add the vanilla and then the eggs, one at a time, beating well after each addition. Fold in the flour.

Spoon the batter into the tin and bake for about 35 minutes. The cake is ready when the side is just beginning to pull away from the tin and a skewer inserted in the middle comes out clean. Let the cake cool in the tin for about 5 minutes before transferring it to a wire rack to cool.

Variations

- FRUIT: Fold through about a cup of raspberries, chopped apple, poached quince (page 175) or any other seasonal fruit after you've added the flour.

- AROMATIC SPICE: Add grated orange zest, ground cinnamon, ginger and nutmeg to the creamed butter and sugar.

- CHOCOLATE: Fold in 1–2 tablespoons of cocoa powder with the flour.

- STREUSEL: Combine $^1/_2$ cup (75 g) plain (all-purpose) flour, $^1/_2$ cup (110 g) demerara sugar, 1 tsp ground cinnamon and 1 cup (150 g) roughly chopped almonds, hazelnuts or walnuts with 100 g ($3^1/_2$ oz) chilled, cubed butter. Work the mixture with your fingertips until it resembles coarse sand. Sprinkle evenly over the cake batter before baking.

RHUBARB *and* VANILLA JAM

My family once commented that this is the best jam I've ever made and, still flush with success from such encouraging feedback, I tend to agree. Tangy, full of rich vanilla flavour and zing from the rhubarb and lemon, it is absolutely gorgeous. A dollop on porridge is a winner, and it's also good stirred through rice pudding (see page 120) or tucked into the little thumbprint biscuits opposite.

MAKES ABOUT 3 CUPS
PREP TIME : 15 MINS, PLUS OVERNIGHT MACERATING
COOK TIME : 20 MINS

600 g (1 lb 5 oz) rhubarb, trimmed and chopped
$2^3/4$ cups (600 g) sugar
$1/2$ cup (125 ml) lemon juice
3 tsp vanilla extract

Combine all the ingredients in a large glass or non-reactive bowl. Stir really well and set aside in a cool place to macerate overnight (this step is important as it softens the rhubarb so you don't have to cook it for as long and lose that fresh, fruity flavour).

The next morning, pop a couple of small plates in the freezer. Sterilise a few jars – I wash mine well in a hot dishwasher, then heat them in a 180°C (350°F) oven for 15 minutes.

Transfer the rhubarb mixture to a saucepan or preserving pan. Cook over high heat, stirring often so it doesn't catch and burn, for about 20 minutes. You'll know it's ready via this little test: take one of your plates out of the freezer and dollop a small spoonful of the hot jam onto it. Carefully run your finger through the middle – if a track is left and the jam looks and acts 'set', it's ready to transfer to jars. If not, keep cooking and test the jam again after a few minutes.

Ladle the jam into the sterilised jars, filling each jar to the top. Tightly seal the jars and invert them onto a board covered with a tea towel (inverting the jars helps create a seal). Store in a cool dark place.

RHUBARB, ORANGE *and* PISTACHIO THUMBPRINTS

These biscuits are little champions – so easy to make, with just the right amount of crumble and, thanks to the ground nuts, they're lovely and moist. Swap the pistachio meal with hazelnut or almond meal and use whatever jam you have handy. Marmalade would be gorgeous, too.

MAKES ABOUT 15-20
PREP TIME : 15 MINS 〉 COOK TIME : 15 MINS

150 g ($5^1/2$ oz) butter, softened
$1/2$ cup (60 g) icing (confectioners') sugar
Grated zest of 1 orange
$2/3$ cup (100 g) plain (all-purpose) flour
$1/2$ cup (60 g) cornflour (cornstarch)
$1/2$ cup (50 g) pistachio meal (see Note)
2–3 Tbsp Rhubarb and vanilla jam (see left)

Preheat the oven to 180°C (350°F). Line two baking trays with baking paper.

Using an electric mixer, beat the butter, icing sugar and orange zest for 5 minutes, until pale and fluffy. Add the flour, cornflour and pistachio meal and mix until well combined.

Roll the dough into walnut-sized balls and place on the trays, leaving room for spreading. Dip the end of a wooden spoon in water, then gently press down in the middle of each dough ball to make a thumb-sized indent (or use your thumb). Fill the cavities with the jam.

Bake the biscuits for 10–15 minutes or until pale golden. Leave them on the trays to cool for a few minutes before transferring them to a wire rack to cool completely.

NOTE

For the pistachio meal, just whizz up about $1/2$ cup (70 g) pistachios in a food processor, or bash until fine using a mortar and pestle.

PEAR, WALNUT *and* NUTMEG CAKE

If this cake were a woman, she'd be Kristin Scott Thomas in The English Patient. *She'd be classy and cultured and effortlessly wear white linen all the time, but also easygoing and not at all precious. Once you've made this cake, I hope you agree that it is indeed a classy, cool number. It's all about the warm spices, the toasted ground nuts and, of course, the understated star of the show, those gorgeous pears.*

This cake is fancy enough for dessert (it's lovely served warm with caramel sauce and definitely with ice cream) or a grown-up morning or afternoon tea. This recipe makes quite a bit of batter so if you don't have a large tin, you could use two 20 cm (8 inch) tins – the cakes may not be as high but you'll have one to enjoy now and one to give away or freeze, so it's a win-win!

SERVES 8

PREP TIME : 25 MINS 〉 COOK TIME : 1 HOUR

2 cups (230 g) walnuts
2/3 cup (110 g) almonds
1 cup (150 g) wholemeal plain
  (all-purpose) flour
1 tsp baking powder
1 1/2 tsp freshly grated nutmeg
1/2 tsp ground cinnamon
1/4 tsp ground cardamom
A pinch of salt

4 pears (not too ripe)
1 Tbsp (20 g) butter, cut into small cubes
1 1/4 cups (275 g) firmly packed brown sugar
1 cup (250 g) unsalted butter, softened
Grated zest of 1 orange
4 eggs
1/2 cup (125 ml) buttermilk or yoghurt
Sweet dukkah (page 161) or chopped nuts,
  to serve

Preheat the oven to 160°C (320°F). Grease and line a 24 cm (9 1/2 inch) cake tin.

Combine the walnuts and almonds on a baking tray and toast for about 10 minutes or until fragrant. Let the nuts cool for a few minutes, then transfer to a food processor and blitz to a coarse meal (or a fine meal, if you prefer a fine-textured cake). Transfer to a bowl and whisk in the flour, baking powder, spices and salt. Set aside.

Peel and halve the pears. Using either a melon baller or a teaspoon, scoop out the seeds and cores. Fill each cavity with a little of the cubed butter. Sprinkle 1/4 cup (55 g) of the brown sugar over the base of the cake tin, then place the pear halves on top, cut side down.

Using an electric mixer, beat the softened butter, orange zest and remaining brown sugar until the sugar has just dissolved. Add the eggs, one at a time, scraping down the side and beating well after each addition. Fold in half of the nut mixture and half of the buttermilk or yoghurt. Mix on low speed and then repeat with the remaining ingredients.

Gently spoon the batter into the tin, being careful not to move the pears, and smooth the top. Bake for 30 minutes, then rotate the tin 180 degrees and bake for another 20 minutes or until it is beginning to pull away from the side of the tin and the middle feels springy.

Let the cake cool in the tin for 20 minutes before gently turning it out onto a serving plate and sprinkling it with sweet dukkah or a few chopped nuts. It's beautiful served warm with some honeyed yoghurt or cream, or just on its own.

HUMMINGBIRD LOAF CAKE

There's a lot going on here: toasted nuts, spices, pineapple and carrot, but it works beautifully together. This cake is so easy to make, lasts well for a few days (tightly wrapped in foil) and is lovely topped with a cream cheese icing and sprinkled with a few of the crumbled candied walnuts from page 58. I also love it toasted in a sandwich press and spread with a little butter.

SERVES 6-8

PREP TIME : 20 MINS ❱ COOK TIME : 40 MINS

2 cups (300 g) wholemeal plain
   (all-purpose) flour
2 tsp baking powder
1 tsp ground cinnamon
1 tsp ground ginger
$^{1}/_{2}$ tsp freshly grated nutmeg
1 cup (220 g) firmly packed brown sugar
$^{3}/_{4}$ cup (185 ml) vegetable oil

4 eggs
2 tsp vanilla extract
$1^{1}/_{2}$ cups (235 g) grated carrot
1 cup (115 g) walnuts, toasted and
   roughly chopped
$1^{1}/_{4}$ cups (200 g) chopped fresh
   or tinned pineapple

Preheat the oven to 180°C (350°F). Grease a 30 x 12 cm (12 x 4$^{1}/_{2}$ inch) loaf tin. Line the tin with baking paper.

Combine the flour, baking powder, spices and brown sugar in a bowl and whisk to remove any lumps. Whisk the oil, eggs and vanilla in a large jug, then fold the wet ingredients into the dry ingredients. Add the carrot, walnuts and pineapple and fold until combined.

Spoon the batter into the tin and smooth the top. Bake for 40 minutes or until the cake feels firm to the touch and is just pulling away from the sides of the tin. Let the cake cool in the tin for about 5 minutes before transferring it to a wire rack to cool.

Sweet dukkah

Sweet dukkah is lovely sprinkled over the pear cake on page 158, but is also good over porridge or a quick breakfast of poached or fresh fruit and natural yoghurt.

Preheat the oven to 180°C (350°F). Toast $^{1}/_{2}$ cup (75 g) hazelnuts on a baking tray for 5 minutes. Add $^{1}/_{3}$ cup (50 g) sesame seeds, 2 Tbsp poppy seeds and $^{1}/_{2}$ tsp coriander seeds and toast for another 5 minutes.

Combine the hazelnuts with $^{2}/_{3}$ cup (100 g) raw unsalted pistachios in a food processor and blitz until the mixture resembles coarse breadcrumbs. Add the toasted seeds, 2 Tbsp brown sugar, $^{1}/_{2}$ tsp ground cardamom, $^{1}/_{2}$ tsp ground cinnamon, $^{1}/_{4}$ tsp freshly grated nutmeg and a pinch of sea salt. Give it a quick blitz, then store in a jar or airtight container. *Makes about 1$^{1}/_{2}$ cups*

CINNAMON *and* FRUIT SCONES

This is probably the recipe I make most at home – generally because scones are the easiest option when you want to make something special for afternoon tea but don't have loads of time to do so. I try to always have a bag of scones in the freezer ready to cook (from frozen, which is handy). It means that the dreaded 'pop in' guests can find themselves in front of piping hot, deliciously aromatic scones within 30 minutes of walking in the door. And that is super satisfying for everyone involved.

MAKES 6–8
PREP TIME : 10 MINS, PLUS 40 MINS RESTING ⁂ COOK TIME : 20 MINS

1 cup (250 g) chilled butter
1¹/3 cups (250 g) dried fruit
1 cup (250 ml) strong hot tea
2¹/3 cups (350 g) plain (all-purpose) flour,
   plus extra for dusting
1 cup (150 g) wholemeal plain (all-purpose)
   flour
¹/4 cup (55 g) caster (superfine) sugar
2 Tbsp baking powder
¹/2 tsp ground cinnamon
A pinch of salt
1¹/3 cups (330 ml) buttermilk

Cinnamon glaze
¹/4 cup (55 g) caster (superfine) sugar
1 tsp ground cinnamon
1 egg
2 Tbsp single (pure) cream

Line a large baking tray with baking paper.

Grate the butter onto a plate and put it in the fridge. Put the dried fruit in a bowl and pour in the tea. Set aside to soak.

Meanwhile, whisk the flours, sugar, baking powder, cinnamon and salt in a large bowl. Add the cold grated butter and rub together (it's fine if the mixture is still lumpy and there are still pea-sized pieces of butter). Pour in the buttermilk and the drained fruit and lightly mix until just combined.

Turn the dough out onto a lightly floured surface and shape it into a large disc about 3 cm (1¼ inches) thick. Cut the dough into rounds using a pastry cutter or a glass, or slice it into wedges, and place on the baking tray. Place the scones in the freezer for at least 40 minutes (or up to a few weeks, tightly wrapped) before baking.

Preheat the oven to 200°C (400°F).

For the glaze, whisk the sugar and cinnamon in a small bowl. In a separate bowl, whisk the egg with the cream. Brush the tops of the frozen scones with the egg and cream mixture, then sprinkle with the cinnamon sugar.

Bake the scones for 20 minutes or until golden brown. Serve warm with jam – the Rhubarb and vanilla jam on page 157 would be perfect.

Variations

Omit the dried fruit and add one of these options when you're combining the wet and dry ingredients.

- ORANGE AND DATE: Add the grated zest of 1 orange and $\frac{1}{2}$ cup (80 g) chopped dates.

- CHOCOLATE CHIP: Add $\frac{2}{3}$ cup (100 g) chocolate chips.

- BLUEBERRY AND LEMON: Add $\frac{2}{3}$ cup (100 g) frozen blueberries and the grated zest of 1 lemon.

- COCONUT AND WHITE CHOCOLATE: Add $\frac{1}{2}$ cup (45 g) desiccated coconut and $\frac{1}{2}$ cup (85 g) white chocolate chips.

- CARDAMOM AND TOASTED ALMOND: Add $\frac{1}{2}$ cup (80 g) roughly chopped toasted almonds and $\frac{1}{2}$ tsp ground cardamom.

FIG *and* ALMOND CAKE
that thinks it's a tart

This is basically a fig frangipane tart without the pastry, so you can feel awesome about eating it because just think of all that butter you haven't had. Also great to know: it's very easy to make, tastes delicious and is the perfect foil for pretty much any seasonal fruit. I love it with raspberries, plums, poached quinces (page 175), apples and figs in particular. Serve it with a scoop of ice cream or a dollop of thick cream.

SERVES 6-8
PREP TIME : 15 MINS 〉 COOK TIME : 40 MINS

1 cup (160 g) almonds
1/3 cup (75 g) caster (superfine) sugar
1/3 cup (50 g) plain (all-purpose) flour
1 tsp baking powder
2 eggs
1/4 cup (60 g) butter, melted
1 tsp vanilla extract
Grated zest of 1 orange
10 figs, halved
1/3 cup (110 g) Rhubarb and vanilla jam (page 157) or strawberry jam

Preheat the oven to 180°C (350°F). Grease a 24 cm (9½ inch) loose-based fluted tart tin (or a spring-form cake tin) really well.

Put the almonds on a baking tray and toast in the oven for 10 minutes. Let the nuts cool, then blitz in a food processor until you have a fine meal. Transfer to a bowl and add the sugar, flour and baking powder. Whisk to combine.

Whisk the eggs, melted butter, vanilla and orange zest together. Fold in the almond mixture, then pour the batter into the tart tin. Arrange the fig halves on top. Bake for 25–30 minutes or until the cake is beginning to pull away from the side of the tin and feels firm to touch.

Just before the cake is ready to come out of the oven, put the jam in a small saucepan over medium heat to soften it. As soon as you take the cake out of the oven, gently brush the jam all over the top. Serve the cake warm or at room temperature.

Easter lunch in the orchard

'Treat your family like company and company like family.' A friend said to me recently that this is her cooking mantra and I immediately adopted it as mine, too. Doesn't everyone want their guests to feel completely welcome and their family to feel that even the simplest meal is a special moment to come together?

That's not to say I spend hours making fancy food every night. I really don't. Because actually, it's not all about the food (hot, tasty and abundant is the aim); it's about how people feel at your table. It's about the candle, the flowers, the cloth napkins and the fact that you have dimmed or turned off the overhead lights. Even a supper of eggs and soldiers can feel special when you light a candle, throw some flowers in a jar and play some happy tunes in the background.

At the time of writing, the world is in shutdown thanks to Covid-19, and the Easter we had planned with my extended family and a table of some 22 cousins, siblings and parents was cancelled. So the four of us stayed home for a special lunch together in the garden. And it was lovely.

Whatever the size of your group, I hope you try this menu one day soon. Give yourself the morning to play your favourite music and potter in the kitchen. Get everyone to bring a table outside and set it prettily, then spend the afternoon grazing, talking and lying in the sun. Afterwards, watch a movie, have toast for dinner and pop off to bed early. Now that's my idea of a perfect day.

Aromatic SLOW-COOKED LAMB SHOULDER

SMOKY GREEN SAUCE *for everything* ❧ PUMPKIN *and* PARMESAN POLENTA

ROASTED CARROTS *with* YOGHURT, HAZELNUTS *and* HARISSA

No-need-to-knead FOCACCIA *(page 187)*

QUINCE FRANGIPANE TART

*It's not all about the food;
it's about how people feel at your table.*

Aromatic SLOW-COOKED LAMB SHOULDER

Aside from it being delicious, the best thing about this lamb is that you can put it on in the morning and head out for a while with the smug knowledge that lunch will be waiting for you when you get home.

SERVES 6
PREP TIME : 20 MINUTES ⚘ COOK TIME : 5³/4 HOURS

1.8–2 kg (4–4 lb 8 oz) lamb shoulder
8 garlic cloves, peeled
2 Tbsp coriander seeds
2 Tbsp cumin seeds
1 Tbsp fennel seeds
1 tsp sea salt
¼ cup (60 ml) olive oil
2 lemons, thinly sliced
2 red onions, sliced
¼ cup (60 ml) pomegranate molasses
2 Tbsp honey
2 Tbsp wholegrain mustard
¼ cup (60 ml) red wine vinegar
¹/3 cup (50 g) toasted pine nuts
¹/3 cup (50 g) pomegranate seeds
1 small handful coriander (cilantro) leaves

Bring the lamb to room temperature and make a few incisions across the top of the meat.

Preheat the oven to 220°C (425°F).

Using a mortar and pestle, pound the garlic, spices and sea salt into a coarse paste. Add the olive oil, then rub the paste over the lamb, pushing it into the incisions as much as possible. Layer the lemon and red onion slices over the base of a roasting tin, then place the lamb on top. Pour ¹/3 cup (80 ml) water into the tin and roast for 30 minutes. Reduce the oven temperature to 120°C (235°F), tightly cover the tin with foil and cook for about 4¹/2 hours or until the lamb is very, very tender.

Towards the end of the cooking time, combine the pomegranate molasses, honey, mustard, vinegar and ¼ cup (60 ml) water in a small saucepan and bring to the boil.

Pour the pomegranate glaze over the lamb. Increase the heat back to 220°C (425°F) and cook, uncovered, for a final 40 minutes or until the lamb skin is beginning to crisp up.

Sprinkle the lamb with the pine nuts, pomegranate seeds and coriander leaves. Spoon the lemon and onion slices over the top to serve.

SMOKY GREEN SAUCE
for everything

Bright and fresh with layers of smoky flavour and just enough saltiness and acid, this sauce comes in handy to pep up everything from a fried egg on toast to a simple veggie and rice bowl, a pasta salad and, in this case, a rich slow-cooked lamb dish.

MAKES ABOUT 2 CUPS (500 ML)
PREP TIME : 5 MINS 〉 COOK TIME : NIL

1 avocado, peeled, stone removed
1 handful mixed herbs, e.g. sorrel, parsley and mint,
    or basil, tarragon and dill
2 Tbsp capers, rinsed
1 Tbsp pure maple syrup
2 chipotle chillies in adobo sauce (see Note)
1/4 cup (60 ml) olive oil
Grated zest and juice of 1 orange

Combine all the ingredients in a food processor or blender and blitz until a smooth sauce forms. Add a little water if you prefer a runnier sauce. Transfer the sauce to a jar and store in the fridge for a couple of days.

NOTE
Chipotle chillies in adobo sauce are little flavour bombs that come in a tin. You'll find them in the Mexican section of the supermarket.

PUMPKIN *and* PARMESAN POLENTA

This rich take on polenta is such a handy recipe to have on hand. It makes a beautiful 'bed' for the slow-cooked lamb, but also for barbecued steaks or, for a vegetarian option, sautéed mushrooms or roasted beetroot with feta cheese, rocket (arugula) and tamari almonds. The mellow flavour of the roasted pumpkin is a winner. You could also use sweet potato.

SERVES 6
PREP TIME : 20 MINS 〉 COOK TIME : 45 MINS

3 cups (450 g) cubed pumpkin
Olive oil, for drizzling
1 1/2 cups (285 g) polenta
75 g (2 1/2 oz) butter, cubed
1 cup (95 g) grated parmesan cheese

Preheat the oven to 180°C (350°F). Place the pumpkin on a baking tray and drizzle with olive oil. Roast for 45 minutes or until the pumpkin is cooked through. Transfer the pumpkin to a food processor or blender and purée until smooth, adding 1/4 cup (60 ml) water to loosen it a little.

While the pumpkin is cooking, bring 4 cups (1 litre) generously salted water to the boil. Whisk in the polenta in a thin, steady stream. Cook over low heat, stirring almost continuously, for 30 minutes or until the polenta is thick and smooth.

Remove the polenta from the heat, stir in the puréed pumpkin, butter and parmesan, and season to taste. Keep the polenta warm until ready to serve. (I do this in a slow cooker, which means the polenta can be prepared hours in advance. If kept on low heat, it keeps cooking very gently and seems to fluff up quite beautifully.)

ROASTED CARROTS *with* YOGHURT, HAZELNUTS *and* HARISSA

This is an insanely tasty dish that's a great side but also brilliant on its own with some warm Turkish bread or tossed greens. Big flavours, easy to put together and using some nice solid seasonal veg to great appeal… yes, please!

SERVES 4-6
PREP TIME : 15 MINS ⸱ COOK TIME : 45 MINS

6 carrots
Olive oil, for drizzling
1¹/₂ cups (390 g) Greek-style yoghurt
1 handful rocket (arugula)
¹/₂ cup (75 g) hazelnuts, roasted and roughly chopped
1 small handful dried rose petals (optional)

Harissa dressing
¹/₄ cup (60 ml) extra virgin olive oil
2 Tbsp harissa, or to taste
Grated zest and juice of 1 lemon

Preheat the oven to 200°C (400°F). Peel and slice the carrots into batons. Arrange on a baking tray, drizzle with olive oil and sprinkle with salt. Roast the carrots for 45 minutes or until cooked through and beginning to caramelise at the edges.

For the harissa dressing, whisk together the olive oil, harissa, lemon zest and juice and season to taste. (Perhaps start with just 1 tablespoon of harissa and add more to taste – some brands are hotter than others.)

To serve, spread the base of a big platter or bowl with the yoghurt, top with the carrots and rocket and then drizzle the dressing over the top. Finish with the hazelnuts and rose petals, if using.

QUINCE FRANGIPANE TART

Possibly my favourite thing to make and share, a good frangipane tart is a thing of beauty and deliciousness. The frangipane refers to a mix of ground almonds, butter, sugar and egg, which is spread on the base of a shortcrust pastry shell, topped with fruit and baked. It looks pretty, tastes beautiful and is all done and dusted (with icing sugar, if you like) well in advance.

A note on the frangipane mixture: it does make a difference to the end result if you toast and grind the almonds fresh, but if you don't have time, almond meal from the shops will work. I also highly recommend doubling the frangipane mixture and freezing half – it's such a handy thing to have stashed away ready to dollop on some frozen puff pastry and top with a bit of fruit for a quick dessert or afternoon tea.

SERVES 6

PREP TIME : 35 MINS, PLUS 1 HOUR CHILLING ❧ COOK TIME : 45 MINS

3 poached quinces (see right), cut into 1 cm (1/2 inch)
   thick slices

Sweet shortcrust pastry
1 1/3 cups (200 g) plain (all-purpose) flour,
   plus extra for dusting
1/3 cup (40 g) icing (confectioners') sugar
A pinch of salt
150 g (5 1/2 oz) chilled unsalted butter,
   cut into small cubes
1/4 cup (60 ml) iced water

Frangipane filling
1/3 cup (80 g) butter, softened
1/2 cup (110 g) caster (superfine) sugar
3/4 cup (120 g) almonds, lightly toasted and ground
1 Tbsp plain (all-purpose) flour
2 Tbsp cornflour (cornstarch)
1 egg
1 tsp vanilla bean paste

To make the pastry, combine the flour, icing sugar and salt on a work surface. Bring into a mound and make a well in the centre. Fill the well with the cubed butter and a splash of the iced water. Use the heels of your hands to bring the mixture together, working the butter into the flour and adding more water as needed. Keep going until you have a rough dough. Shape into a disc, cut off a quarter of the pastry and shape it into a smaller disc, then wrap both and place in the fridge to rest for 30 minutes.

Lightly dust your work surface with flour, then roll out the larger disc of pastry into a round about 3 mm (⅛ inch) thick. Gently drape the pastry over your rolling pin and ease it into a loose-based fluted tart tin, 23 cm (9 inches) in diameter and 3 cm (1¼ inches) deep. Press the pastry down into the crease where the base meets the side. Cut away the excess pastry to create a nice neat edge. Pop it into the fridge for another 30 minutes.

Preheat the oven to 200°C (400°F). Prick the base of the pastry a few times with a fork. Line with baking paper and fill with pastry weights, uncooked rice or dried beans. Blind bake for 10 minutes, then remove the weights and baking paper and bake for another 10 minutes or until the pastry looks pale and dry.

For the frangipane, cream the butter and sugar until pale and fluffy. Add the ground almonds, flour, cornflour, egg and vanilla and mix until soft and smooth. Spoon the frangipane into the tart shell and smooth it out to cover the base. Arrange the poached quince slices on top.

Roll out the remaining pastry on a lightly floured work surface. Cut it into ten or so long strips. Place five of the strips across the top of the tart and then weave the remaining strips through them to create a lattice pattern.

Pop the tart into the oven for 25 minutes or until the pastry is golden brown. Serve the tart warm or at room temperature with thick (double) cream or ice cream.

Variation

This recipe can be adapted to suit any time of year. Try swapping the quinces with dollops of marmalade or jam. Poached pears are also beautiful, as are fresh raspberries or apricots.

Poached quinces

Combine 1 cup (220 g) sugar, 3 cups (750 ml) water and 1 teaspoon vanilla bean paste in a large saucepan. Cook over high heat, whisking every now and then until the sugar dissolves. Meanwhile, peel and core 4 quinces, then cut into wedges and add to the sugar syrup. Cut a circle of baking paper to fit just inside the pan and press it down on the surface of the syrup. Cover the pan and cook over low heat for 3 hours or until the quinces are ruby red and soft. *Makes 4 (which is a little more than the tart recipe requires, but I'm sure the leftovers will find good use!)*

Autumn feast

The sight of a golden fish pie surrounded by a few tasty salads really makes my heart (and tummy) sing! You could make this lovely menu for a birthday dinner, a family lunch or perhaps a Good Friday feast.

None of these dishes are difficult, although they ask for a little time, but I promise they'll repay your efforts with a really tasty, memorable lunch... just like this one, on a perfect clear autumn day at Logan Brae Orchard in the Blue Mountains. This is one of my absolute favourite places in the world. Dad used to bring us here to pick apples as kids and the old packing shed shop is still full of good smells of hot apple pies, mulled apple juice and boxes upon boxes of crisp apples ready to walk out the door. And then there's that view – located on the edge of the Shipley Plateau, the orchard drops away to valleys and the most incredible escarpment view.

These days the orchard is also home to the Upward family: Asia and Sam and their daughters, Grace and baby Isla (and a menagerie of curious sheep, alpacas and chooks). The Upwards live in the original 100-year-old weatherboard cottage, surrounded by some of the first apple trees planted some 80 years ago. Every weekend they open up their stunning B&B, host weddings and welcome families like mine who come to buy apples and gawp at the view. On a sunny autumn Tuesday, they took a rare afternoon off, invited some friends over and let me bring fish pie and salads and cake so we could all stop for a while, sit in the orchard, sip sparkling cider and share a simple and tasty feast in the sun.

Asia's tips to make entertaining easy

I like to have everything prepped and made before my guests walk through the door. I also don't want to be standing in the kitchen plating up so I make dishes that can go straight on the table where everyone can help themselves. This means that when our guests arrive, all that's left to do is pour them a drink and chat. I'd also say that entertaining during the day is easier with children, or simply having someone over for an afternoon drink and cheese platter. That way I get to sit and enjoy my time with them without mountains of organising.

@loganbraeorchard

FISH PIE ⟩ PICKLE SALAD
GREMOLATA TABOULEH
Gran's ALMOND CAKE *(page 105)*
with FIG *and* GINGER COMPOTE

This memorable lunch was enjoyed on a perfect clear autumn day in the Blue Mountains.

FISH PIE

I love how this pie is shaped like a giant Easter egg! It's the perfect dish to serve on Good Friday if eating fish that day is something you observe. But don't save it for just one day of the year – this pie is wonderful for a picnic, to take to a friend or for an easy meal any day.

The idea for shaping and cutting the pie like this comes from one of my favourite books, Salt and Time *by Alissa Timoshkina. And speaking of time, please give yourself plenty to make this, because if you do the filling the night before or at least a few hours ahead and it's nice and cold when you come to assembly, it's much easier to handle.*

SERVES 6-8

PREP TIME : 30 MINS, PLUS CHILLING ⟩ COOK TIME : ABOUT 1 HOUR

1 leek
2 cups (500 ml) full-cream milk
400 g (14 oz) ling or other firm white fish, pin-boned
300 g (10½ oz) salmon or trout, pin-boned
1½ Tbsp (30 g) butter
¼ cup (35 g) plain (all-purpose) flour
400 g (14 oz) hot-smoked trout or salmon

1 quantity Sour cream pastry (page 144)
4 hard-boiled eggs, quartered
½ cup (50 g) flaked almonds, toasted
About 1 cup soft herbs, finely chopped (I use a mixture of parsley, dill and sorrel)
Grated zest of 1 lemon
1 egg
2 Tbsp single (pure) cream

Wash the leek well, then finely chop the white and green parts. Put the green part in a deep-sided frying pan with the milk and a good grinding of black pepper. Heat until just at boiling point. Add the ling and salmon, cover and simmer for 5 minutes. Turn off the heat and set aside for 5 minutes. Check the fish is just cooked through, then transfer it to a plate.

Strain the milk, discarding the leek. Wipe out the pan and place it over medium–high heat. Add the butter and the white part of the leek and cook for a few minutes or until the leek has softened. Add the flour and cook for a minute or so, stirring well to make a thick paste. Pour in a little of the warm milk and stir until the mixture thickens. Gradually add the remaining milk and cook, stirring, until you have a thick sauce.

Break up the ling, salmon and the smoked trout and gently fold it into the sauce. Season well with salt and pepper and pop it into the fridge to cool completely.

Meanwhile, make the pastry according to the recipe, removing a third of the pastry and wrapping it separately. Chill both wrapped pastry portions for 30 minutes.

Roll out the larger pastry portion on a lightly floured surface into a large oval, about 3 mm (⅛ inch) thick. Gently fold the chopped egg, flaked almonds, herbs and lemon zest into the fish mixture. Spread the mixture over the pastry, leaving a 3 cm (1¼ inch) border.

Roll out the remaining pastry into a smaller oval and drape it over the top of the filling. Crimp the pastry edges together so you have a dome-shaped pie. Re-roll any pastry trimmings and cut out shapes to decorate the top of your pie. Pop the pie into the fridge for 30 minutes (or up to a few hours until you're ready to cook it).

Preheat the oven to 200°C (400°F). Whisk the egg and cream together, brush it over the pie and sprinkle the pie with a little sea salt. Bake for 35–40 minutes or until the pastry is golden brown. Serve the pie hot, warm or at room temperature. Delicious!

GREMOLATA TABOULEH

This is my fusion of that bright-green garnish for rich, slow-cooked dishes like osso buco, with the classic parsley and burghul salad. The result is a big-flavoured side dish that peps up any meal. I have read that parsley is full of vitamins and antioxidants, so feel very worthy when we have this on the table! Here, with the fish pie and the pickle salad, it's a bright side note with punchy greens and flavours. I love it for lunch, too, with some tuna or in a wrap with haloumi or feta.

SERVES 4
PREP TIME : 15 MINS, PLUS 20 MINUTES STANDING
COOK TIME : NIL

2 tomatoes
1 cup (175 g) fine burghul
Grated zest and juice of 2 lemons
3 garlic cloves, finely chopped
3 spring onions (scallions), finely chopped
1/2 cup mint leaves, finely chopped
2 cups parsley leaves, finely chopped
1/4 cup (60 ml) olive oil
Pomegranate seeds (optional)

Finely chop the tomatoes, retaining the juices. Transfer to a bowl with the burghul, lemon zest, lemon juice and garlic and mix well. Set aside for 20 minutes or so – the lemon juice will 'cook' and soften the burghul.

Add the remaining ingredients and gently toss to combine. Season the salad with salt and freshly ground black pepper.

NOTE
You can replace the burghul with couscous or cracked wheat that has been cooked until al dente.

PICKLE SALAD

This is a sort of Russian salad but without the mayonnaise and with more pickle than fresh vegetables – being an enormous fan of pickles of all kinds, I love them in a salad. This would also be great alongside the Porchetta on page 16. I like to add some left-over poached or roasted chicken to the salad mixture to use as a sandwich filling or pile on top of toasted sourdough.

SERVES 4-6
PREP TIME : 10 MINS 〉 COOK TIME : 5 MINS

1 cup (140 g) frozen peas
5 pickled cucumbers, finely chopped, brine reserved
2 carrots, peeled and finely chopped
1/2 red onion, very thinly sliced
1 cup (115 g) walnuts, toasted and roughly chopped
Juice of 1 lemon
1 Tbsp dijon mustard
1/4 cup (65 g) crème fraîche or sour cream
1/4 cup (70 g) Greek-style yoghurt
2 Tbsp dill, finely chopped

Cook the peas in a small saucepan of boiling water until just tender. Drain and run under cold water so they keep their lovely green colour.

Combine the peas, pickled cucumber, carrot, red onion and walnuts in a bowl.

Whisk 1/3 cup (80 ml) of the reserved pickle brine with the lemon juice, mustard, crème fraîche and yoghurt. Gently toss the dressing with the vegetable mixture. Sprinkle with the dill and chill until serving.

Fig and ginger compote

This is a lovely spicy autumn compote that looks and tastes gorgeous spooned over Gran's almond cake (page 105).

Combine 6–8 figs, 2 Tbsp brown sugar, 2 tsp grated ginger and the juice of 1 lemon in a saucepan. Split a vanilla bean lengthways and scrape the seeds into the pan, then add the scraped pod. Add 1/3 cup (80 ml) water and cook over medium heat, stirring often, for 10 minutes or until the figs are completely collapsed. Remove from the heat and serve warm or store in the fridge for up to a week. *Makes about 1 cup*

Loaves and fishes

Country cooks are, in my experience, infinitely creative, unflappable, thrifty and terrific at meal planning. They are masters of the 'loaves and fishes' meal or, in other words, have an enviable ability to pull together beautiful big meals with minimal fuss. The most obvious reason for this is that when you live an hour or two from a supermarket, you quickly learn to have a well-stocked freezer, pantry and vegetable garden, and know what to do with them.

Having lived in the country for some 15 years now, I am learning this great life skill, but still regularly run out of essentials and reprimand myself for failing to nail any kind of long-term meal plan.

One example of a true loaves and fishes queen, though, is Annabelle Hickson. She lives a good 40 minutes from town (Tenterfield, in far-northern New South Wales) on a pecan farm with her husband Ed and their children Daisy, Tom and Harriet. She's also a talented writer, photographer, stylist and, more recently, publisher and creator of *Galah* magazine. And she makes meals and gatherings come together with such a relaxed style that it's a joy to behold.

My husband Tim and I joined the Hicksons for dinner on a cool autumn evening. We sat around their lovely table well after the children had pottered off to bed, enjoying that beautiful time after a good meal when the candles are burning low and the conversation is bubbling along happily.

Annabelle's advice on having people over

Over the years I have become more and more relaxed about having people over. This softening can be put down to practice (anything you do over and over again becomes easier) and personal exhaustion. I am too tired to get too worked up. But no matter how lazy I feel, I can still summon the energy to put a white linen tablecloth on the normally chaotic kitchen table, set it with my grandmother's special plates and dot little ceramic ink wells and old tomato tins filled with flowers down the middle of the table. Just simple flowers – nothing too high or grand – just plonked. It takes five minutes and looks beautiful and signifies to me, the children and the guests that there is something special about coming together for a meal.

@annabellehickson

AMARO SPRITZ

No-need-to-knead FOCACCIA SQUARES
with honeycomb, parmesan, pecans and olives

GENTLY SPICED VENISON OSSO BUCO *with sweet potato purée*

ROASTED BROCCOLINI *with seeds*

Annabelle's QUINCE *and* PECAN ICE CREAM

*When you live an hour or two from a supermarket,
you quickly learn to have a well-stocked freezer,
pantry and vegetable garden.*

Amaro spritz

Move over, Aperol spritz – your amaro cousin is coming to stay. I much prefer this beverage to its bright-orange counterpart; it's not nearly as sweet ('amaro' means 'bitter' in Italian) and it feels fun and fancy. Make it up in individual glasses or a jug.

For each person, combine 1 shot (30 ml/1 fl oz) of amaro and the same quantity of soda water with ¼ cup (60 ml) sparkling wine and a slice of lime. Stir to combine. Serve with lots of ice.

No-need-to-knead FOCACCIA SQUARES

I lived in Northern Italy for a few years in my twenties and it never failed to delight me when my drink arrived with a little bowl of potato chips, a plate of crostini spread with butter and topped with an anchovy or, best of all, a plate of warm focaccia squares, all golden and salty and delicious. A platter of warm focaccia squares is still my favourite thing to serve with drinks before dinner. And to make it really fancy, I arrange them on a big platter with some beautiful goat's curd or a hard cheese like parmesan, a hunk of honeycomb and some pecans and olives.

MAKES 1 LARGE RECTANGULAR LOAF
PREP TIME : 25 MINS, PLUS OVERNIGHT PROVING } COOK TIME : 25 MINS

2 tsp (14 g) dry yeast
2 tsp sugar
2¹/2 cups (625 ml) lukewarm water
¹/2 cup (125 ml) olive oil, plus extra
  for drizzling

4 cups (600 g) plain (all-purpose)
  flour
¹/4 cup (35 g) sea salt flakes

Whisk together the yeast, sugar and lukewarm water in a large bowl and leave for 10 minutes to get nice and frothy.

Add the oil, flour and 1 tablespoon of the sea salt flakes to the yeast mixture and stir until just combined (or, as I love to do, use your hands to mix it together). It will look like a big shaggy mess and that's just what you want. Cover the bowl and put it in the fridge all day or overnight, or until it's bubbled up nicely and doubled in size. Twice throughout this process, take the dough out of the fridge and give it a few turns, folding it in over itself with the edges of your hands, then cover it and pop it back into the fridge. You can do this fermentation step on the benchtop if you prefer – it should take between 2 and 4 hours for the dough to double up, depending on the temperature of your kitchen.

Generously oil a 32 x 24 cm (12¹/2 x 9¹/2 inch) baking tray (or thereabouts – the thinner the focaccia is, the crunchier it will be). Give your dough a few turns, bringing it together into a ball, then gently press it into the baking tray so it reaches towards the edges. Leave the dough to rise, uncovered, in a moderately warm kitchen for 45 minutes.

Now for the fun part! With your fingers, press divets into the dough (gently, though – don't break the dough surface). Whisk ¹/4 cup (60 ml) water with 1 tablespoon of the sea salt flakes and pour the brine over the top of the dough, letting it pool in the divets here and there. Set the dough aside for another 45 minutes. (Thank you to my baking hero, Samin Nosrat, for the idea of pouring a brine mixture over the focaccia at the last proving – this is what helps it develop such a crunchy, golden crust on baking.)

Preheat the oven to 220°C (425°F). Sprinkle the last tablespoon of sea salt flakes over the dough. Bake for 25 minutes or until the focaccia is golden. Drizzle some olive oil over the top and let the focaccia cool for a few minutes before cutting it into cubes and serving it warm.

GENTLY SPICED VENISON OSSO BUCO
with sweet potato purée

My husband Tim has been farming red deer for almost 20 years, running them on our hilly property just behind Orange's Mount Canobolas. I've been around for 15 of those years and for much of this time we spent our Saturdays at farmers' markets in Sydney and the Central West. One of the most popular cuts we sold, especially in cooler months, was venison osso buco and this was the recipe I'd print onto cards to send home with our customers. Each piece of osso buco is browned, then braised slowly in an aromatic mixture of spices, tomatoes and onions.

If you can't get your hands on venison, this recipe would also be beautiful with beef osso buco. Ask your butcher to cut it into pieces for you.

SERVES 4–6
PREP TIME : 30 MINS ⸙ COOK TIME : 4 HOURS

1 kg (2 lb 4 oz) osso buco, cut into pieces around 3–4 cm (1¼–1½ inches) thick
⅓ cup (50 g) plain (all-purpose) flour
⅓ cup (80 ml) olive oil
2 brown onions, finely chopped
4 garlic cloves, finely chopped
3 cm (1¼ inch) piece ginger, peeled and finely chopped
2 Tbsp spice mix (page 210) or 1 tsp each of ground cumin and cinnamon and ½ tsp each of ground cardamom and coriander
800 g (1 lb 12 oz) tin whole peeled Italian tomatoes
2 Tbsp tomato paste (concentrated purée)

2 cups (500 ml) chicken or beef stock
3 bay leaves
¼ cup (60 ml) tamari or soy sauce
2 Tbsp brown sugar
Grated zest and juice of 2 limes
1 handful parsley leaves, roughly chopped
1 handful mint leaves, roughly chopped
3 spring onions (scallions), finely chopped

Sweet potato purée
3 large sweet potatoes, peeled and cut into cubes
¼ cup (60 g) unsalted butter
2 Tbsp tamari or soy sauce

Preheat the oven to 140°C (275°F).

Dust the osso buco pieces in the flour. Heat the olive oil in a large heavy-based saucepan over medium–high heat. Brown the osso buco in batches, cooking on each side for a few minutes or until lovely and brown, then transfer to a deep roasting tin.

Reduce the heat under your saucepan and add a splash more olive oil. Cook the onion, stirring, for about 5 minutes or until soft and translucent. Add the garlic, ginger and spice mix and cook for another few minutes.

Add the tomatoes, tomato paste, stock and bay leaves. Add the tamari, brown sugar, lime zest and lime juice. Taste and adjust the seasoning, if needed.

Bring the mixture to a gentle simmer, then pour it over the osso buco pieces. Tightly cover the roasting tin with foil and bake for 3–4 hours or until the meat is lovely and tender and just beginning to fall away from the bone.

About half an hour before the osso buco is ready, make the sweet potato purée. Place the sweet potato in a large saucepan of cold water. Bring to the boil and cook for 15 minutes or until completely tender. Drain and transfer to a food processor with the butter, tamari and some freshly ground black pepper. Blitz until you have a smooth purée.

Sprinkle the osso buco with the chopped herbs and spring onion and serve with the sweet potato purée.

Variations

If you have any leftovers, pull the meat away from the bones and flake it into the braising liquid. Spoon it into small ovenproof bowls, top with puff pastry and bake until golden. Or fold the meat and braising liquid through some pappardelle.

You could also make this dish with lamb shanks. Try to find small shanks and prepare them as per the osso buco.

ROASTED BROCCOLINI
with seeds

This is a really easy, bright and tasty complement to the rich osso buco dish, but is also delicious served on its own with a poached or fried egg, perhaps for lunch.

SERVES 4–6
PREP TIME : 5 MINS ❯ COOK TIME : 10 MINS

3 bunches broccolini, bases trimmed
1/3 cup (55 g) mixed seeds, e.g. sunflower seeds and pepitas (pumpkin seeds)
2 Tbsp tamari or soy sauce

Preheat the oven to 180°C (350°F). Place the broccolini on a baking tray in a single layer. Spread the seeds on another baking tray and drizzle them with the tamari.

Place both trays in the oven for about 10 minutes or until the broccolini is bright green and cooked through but still has lots of crunch. Sprinkle the tamari seed mixture over the broccolini and serve warm.

Annabelle's QUINCE *and* PECAN ICE CREAM

This recipe, and these words, come straight from Annabelle: 'If you are out of eggs or don't have an ice-cream machine, this cheat's no-churn is a saviour. I originally saw it in Nigella Lawson's Nigellissima *as a coffee version, but I now use the cream and condensed milk base as a foundation for whatever I have. I make it with roasted apricots and amaretti liqueur in summer or, here in autumn, with poached quinces and pecans and a lovely pecan liqueur that's made in Glen Gowrie Distillery at Glen Innes, just down the road.'*

MAKES 4 CUPS (1 LITRE)
PREP TIME : 20 MINS, PLUS OVERNIGHT FREEZING ❧ COOK TIME : 5 MINS

600 ml (21 fl oz) single (pure) cream
400 g (14 oz) tin sweetened condensed milk
2 Tbsp pecan liqueur, whiskey or rum
    (the alcohol tastes great but it also
    keeps the ice cream soft)
3 poached quinces (page 175), roughly
    chopped, plus 1 cup (250 ml) of the
    poaching liquid, to serve

Sugared pecans
2¹/₂ cups (250 g) pecans, roughly chopped
2 Tbsp caster (superfine) sugar
A pinch of salt

For the sugared pecans, line a baking tray with baking paper. Put the pecans in a saucepan with the sugar and salt. Cook over medium heat, swirling the pan as you go, until the sugar has melted and coated the nuts. (Nothing happens for so long, until it suddenly does. And that moment of action comes just before the nuts burn, so you have to keep on your toes.) Spread the nuts over the tray and leave to set.

Line a 4 cup (1 litre) loaf tin or container with plastic wrap. Combine the cream with the condensed milk in the bowl of an electric mixer fitted with the whisk attachment and whisk until soft peaks form. Fold in the sugared pecans (reserve a few to sprinkle on top at the end), liqueur and quince pieces, gently pour into the tin or container and freeze overnight.

To serve, scoop the ice cream into bowls, drizzle with the quince poaching liquid and sprinkle with the reserved sugared pecans.

Variation

If you have eggs but no condensed milk, here is a traditional ice-cream base (which is lovely but does require an ice-cream machine).

Gently heat 600 ml (21 fl oz) single (pure) cream in a saucepan until it reaches boiling point, then set aside to cool. Whisk 6 egg yolks with 1 cup (220 g) caster (superfine) sugar until pale and fluffy. Slowly pour in the warm cream, whisking as you go. Pour the mixture into the clean saucepan and stir over low heat until thickened enough to coat the back of the spoon.

Pour the mixture into a cold bowl or jug. When completely cool, churn in an ice-cream machine until it begins to set, then add the sugared pecans and chopped poached quince (there's no need to add the alcohol, other than for the taste!). Churn the ice cream until firm, then transfer to a container and freeze until serving.

WINTER

There's nothing nicer than a good ploughman's picnic lunch – just add sunshine and give yourselves plenty of time to graze away the afternoon.

Narnie's apple pie epitomises exactly what this book is about: families and friends coming together over food and food traditions.

Be good company by bringing something small to say 'thanks for having me': a jar of jam, some flavoured salts or a bottle of cocktail mix. Your friends will love the gesture.

The best thing about curry night? All the heavy lifting is done well in advance, the recipes can be doubled or quadrupled with no problem and everyone loves curry!

Ease the bleak midwinter

Winter can drag on a bit, don't you think? We've all been huddled up at home for too long and even though it's still freezing, we'll take any opportunity to get out or have friends over. And I promise, if you make any of the dishes in this menu, the party will be off to a cracking start!

There's the golden Winter sun soup for ladling into deep bowls and sharing on laps around a fire pit or on the couch in front of a movie with your buddies. And then there's the Fried chicken with hot honey butter and Creamed green curry corn, which truly is one of the yummiest things you'll ever cook and always a big hit.

I recently prepared this menu for my cousin Annie, her partner Darren and their kids, Laura and Nick. These four are a special family and much loved by mine, so it was a pleasure to cook for them and their friends on a freezing winter night. We stood around the fire pit, gorgeous Laura and Nick had friends over and it was loads of fun. Then, being young and cool as they are, the young people went out for the night and Annie and I retired to the couch to watch a movie and share the lemon curd pudding straight out of the oven. Perfection.

Laura's thoughts on entertaining

For me, happiness is sitting with fun people, with candles of all shapes and sizes on the table, drinking bubbles and listening to Norah Jones, and the smell of a yummy warm dinner cooking in the next room. That's the dream for me, so when I'm entertaining I want my guests to feel cosy, warm and welcome. Nothing beats candlelight (a dimmer switch is second best). Also, nothing screams a party better than bunting and some good hanging courtyard lights.

@_lauraagardner
@pavilioncottages
@_anniethinggoes

WINTER SUN SOUP ❧ FRIED CHICKEN *with hot honey butter*
Creamed GREEN CURRY CORN
Granny Mary's self-saucing LEMON CURD PUDDING

*When winter is dragging on, we'll take any opportunity
to get out or have friends over.*

WINTER SUN SOUP

I've named this miso pumpkin soup 'Winter sun soup' because it reminds me of a ray of sunshine in midwinter when we need it most. It's easy, sunny and delicious. A bowl of this soup with a little plate of goat's cheese and warm bread, and perhaps some roasted broccolini (page 189) or a crunchy green salad on the side would make a beautiful wintery lunch or dinner.

SERVES 6 AS A STARTER
PREP TIME : 15 MINS ⁑ COOK TIME : 40 MINS

1 Tbsp ghee or oil
2 brown onions, finely diced
3 garlic cloves, finely chopped
4 cm (1¹/₂ inch) piece ginger, peeled and
    roughly chopped
1 tsp ground turmeric
¹/₂ tsp ground cumin
4 cups (600 g) cubed pumpkin
4 cups (1 litre) chicken or vegetable stock
2 Tbsp white miso
Juice of 2 lemons
Chopped red chilli or chilli flakes,
    to serve (optional)

Seed sprinkle
1²/₃ cups (250 g) mixed seeds, e.g. sesame seeds,
    pepitas (pumpkin seeds) and sunflower seeds
2 Tbsp soy sauce
A pinch of cayenne pepper
1 tsp olive oil

For the seed sprinkle, preheat the oven to 180°C (350°F). Combine the seeds, soy sauce, cayenne pepper and olive oil in a small bowl. Spread the mixture over a baking tray and pop it into the oven for 15 minutes or until the seeds are golden brown.

Meanwhile, melt the ghee or oil in a large saucepan over medium–high heat. Cook the onion, stirring often, for about 10 minutes or until soft. Add the garlic and ginger and cook for a few more minutes.

Add the turmeric, cumin and pumpkin and cook for another minute, stirring to coat the pumpkin with the spices. Pour in the stock and stir well, then bring to a simmer and cook for about 20 minutes or until the pumpkin is completely soft and cooked through. Remove from the heat and cool slightly.

Blitz the soup in batches until lovely and smooth. Stir in the miso and lemon juice and adjust the seasoning to taste.

Serve the soup topped with chilli, if using, and the seed sprinkle.

FRIED CHICKEN
with hot honey butter

I challenge anyone not to feel loved and cheery when a plate of this goodness is put before them. My own kids literally hum with pleasure on the odd occasions that fried chicken is on the menu.

There's a restaurant in Chicago called Honey Butter that specialises in fried chicken doused in honey butter served with corn cakes and creamed corn and green curry. I once heard the restaurant's founder talk about this dish on a podcast and I've been dreaming about it ever since. Because I live in country Australia, not Chicago, I've had to make it up myself and this is the result. So thank you, Honey Butter, for the idea. I have to say it really is the most delicious treat and teenagers particularly seem to love it.

Like the chicken pie in my book A Basket by the Door, this dish is a labour of love and it does take a little time to bring together… the kind of time you might have on a freezing winter afternoon while the fire is going, your couch potatoes are watching movies and one other family is coming over for dinner. (I say 'one other family' because frying food for more than a small group can be a bit of a fiddle.) When making this dish for more than the four of us, I always make it a couple of hours in advance so the mess is well and truly out of the way. If you're doing this, let the fried chicken cool completely on a rack, then wrap it in some paper towel and place it in a container in the fridge. Simply reheat the chicken in a hot oven when you're ready to serve.

A note on thermometers: if you can, use two thermometers for this recipe – a sugar thermometer to gauge the temperature of the oil and a probe thermometer to jab into the chicken to ensure it's cooked through. This isn't essential, but it does take so much of the guesswork out of the process.

SERVES 6-8
PREP TIME : 30 MINS, PLUS OVERNIGHT BRINING 〉 COOK TIME : ABOUT 35 MINS

3/4 cup (165 g) salt
1/4 cup (55 g) sugar
6 chicken drumsticks, skin on
6 chicken thigh cutlets, skin on
About 4 cups (1 litre) vegetable oil, for frying (I use canola oil)
2 cups (500 ml) buttermilk
2 tsp baking powder
1 cup (150 g) plain (all-purpose) flour
1/2 cup (60 g) cornflour (cornstarch)

1 tsp smoked paprika
1 tsp ground cumin
1 tsp sea salt
1 tsp freshly ground black pepper
2 spring onions (scallions), green part only, chopped

Hot honey butter
100 g (3 1/2 oz) unsalted butter
1/3 cup (115 g) honey
Chilli flakes, to taste

Start by brining the chicken a day ahead. Pour 12 cups (3 litres) water into a large saucepan. Add the salt and sugar and bring to the boil. Turn off the heat and leave the brine to cool to room temperature. Add the chicken pieces and refrigerate overnight or for up to 24 hours.

The next day, start by getting everything you need out on the bench. Line a baking tray with a couple of paper towels. Line two roasting tins with baking paper and place a wire rack in or on top of each. Pour the oil into a large flameproof casserole dish or heavy-based saucepan and put it on the stovetop. You'll also need a pair of tongs.

Whisk the buttermilk and baking powder together in one shallow bowl, and combine the flour, cornflour, paprika, cumin, sea salt and pepper in another.

Preheat the oven to 180°C (350°F).

Remove the chicken from the brine and pat dry. Dredge one piece of chicken in the flour mixture, then dip it in the buttermilk and place it on one of the wire racks. Repeat with the remaining chicken pieces. Then, starting with the first piece, dredge each chicken piece in the flour mixture again. (Try not to make the coating too thick or it will stop the chicken from cooking through.)

Turn the heat under the pan of oil to high. Once the oil reaches 175°C (347°F) on a sugar thermometer, it's ready to start frying. If you don't have a thermometer, toss a small piece of bread into the hot oil; if it bubbles straight up to the surface and cooks quickly, the oil is ready.

Fry the chicken pieces in batches for about 5 minutes on each side. Place on the paper towel for a minute or so to absorb the excess oil, then transfer to the wire racks in the roasting tins. Pop the fried chicken into the oven for 15 minutes or until it reaches about 74°C (165°F) on a probe thermometer, to ensure that all the chicken is cooked through and nice and warm when ready to serve. Use this time to do a quick clean up and make the honey butter.

For the honey butter, combine the butter, honey and chilli flakes in a small saucepan over low heat. Stir until the mixture comes together in a glossy sauce.

When ready to serve, pour the honey butter over the fried chicken pieces and sprinkle with the spring onion. Serve with the Creamed green curry corn (page 203).

Recipe pictured page 202

Creamed GREEN CURRY CORN

Yes, I know this sounds a bit unusual. But trust me, it's absolutely delicious. I highly recommend making a double batch and using any leftovers in the best toasted sandwich you'll ever have.

SERVES 6–8
PREP TIME : 10 MINS ⟩ COOK TIME : 10 MINS

1 Tbsp ghee or butter
1 lemongrass stalk, white part bruised and halved lengthways
1 tsp finely grated ginger
2 spring onions (scallions), white part only, finely chopped
3 cups (450 g) fresh or frozen corn kernels
1/2 cup (125 ml) coconut milk
Grated zest and juice of 1 lime
1 cup (250 ml) green curry sauce (see Note)

Melt the ghee or butter in a large frying pan over medium heat. Add the lemongrass, ginger and spring onion. Cook for a few minutes or until the spring onion is completely soft. Add the corn kernels, coconut milk, lime zest and lime juice and cook for 5 minutes or until the corn is tender. Remove and discard the lemongrass pieces.

Transfer three-quarters of the corn mixture to a blender and blitz for a few seconds so you have a rough paste. Combine the paste with the remaining corn mixture and transfer to a serving bowl.

Pour the curry sauce over the corn, to taste, and gently swirl to combine.

NOTE
For the green curry sauce, use the recipe on page 213, but replace the red curry paste with green curry paste.

Granny Mary's self-saucing
LEMON CURD PUDDING

If you don't have a lemon pudding recipe in your repertoire, then here's one to try. This is my hands-down, all-time favourite dessert. If someone you love has had a particularly bad day, having this after (or for!) dinner could be a really good idea. Serve it straight from the baking dish with a jug of cold cream, ideally by a fire, on the couch.

I have named this recipe after my paternal grandmother, who would often have the whole family over for roast lamb on Sundays. Dessert was always either floating islands or hot lemon pudding. Guess which one I loved most?

SERVES 6
PREP TIME : 15 MINS ⟩ COOK TIME : 35 MINS

2^1/$_2$ Tbsp (50 g) butter, softened, plus extra for greasing
^{3}/$_4$ cup (165 g) caster (superfine) sugar
1 tsp vanilla bean paste
Grated zest and juice of 3 lemons – you'll need ^{1}/$_2$ cup (125 ml) lemon juice
3 eggs, separated
1 cup (250 ml) full-cream milk
^{1}/$_3$ cup (50 g) plain (all-purpose) flour

Preheat the oven to 170°C (340°F). Grease a 6 cup (1.5 litre) ovenproof dish with butter.

Combine the butter, sugar, vanilla and lemon zest in a food processor or blender and blitz for a few seconds. Add the lemon juice, egg yolks, milk and flour and blitz again so you have a smooth batter.

Whisk the egg whites until stiff peaks form, then gradually fold them into the batter.

Spoon the batter into the greased dish and smooth the top. Gently place the dish in a roasting tin and very carefully pour in enough hot water to come halfway up the side of the dish. Bake the pudding on the middle rack of the oven for 35 minutes or until it is golden and has bubbled up beautifully.

Serve the warm pudding with cold cream or vanilla ice cream.

NOTE

When I make this pudding, I do everything a few hours in advance and leave the pudding, covered, in a cold spot in the pantry or laundry. Just as we are sitting down to our main meal, I pop it into the oven. This means that all the washing up is done and dusted (and to be fair, there's quite a bit in this recipe). You do sacrifice a little bit of fluff and height by not cooking it straight away, but it really doesn't make enough of a difference to bother anyone.

Curry night

For me, having friends over in the middle of winter means absolutely everything is done well in advance, ready to be reheated or bubbling away quietly (and aromatically) in a low oven before the first knock on the door. This is mostly because our house is small and I can't deal with cooking and mess while everyone's hanging around the kitchen, but also because I don't want to miss any of the chat.

The other big bonus of the 'curry night' is that you can so easily delegate various dishes and share the cooking with friends for a big family-style meal. I did just that for this meal, co-cooking with my friend Kate McKay at her place in Collector, New South Wales for a wintery Friday night with friends. I made the lamb dish, Kate made the cauliflower one and both of us took care of the rest together before everyone arrived. We caught up over the roti dough, sipped some beautiful Collector Wines chardonnay (made by her clever winemaker brother-in-law, Alex), listened to good music and chopped and stirred and laughed. Actually, I think cooking with a friend, when there's no big rush or stress, is one of life's great joys.

Kate's kitchen happens to be one of my favourite rooms in the world. It's something to do with all the art on the walls, the beautiful old dresser full of Kate's bowls, mugs and plates (she's a talented ceramicist) plus other pieces and curiosities, the warmth of the pot-belly stove in the corner and the memories of many happy meals at her table.

Disclaimer: this collection of recipes is not at all authentic, but they are all very easy and tasty!

Kate's tips for being well prepared

I like to have the end of the party taken care of well before start time because I take my eye off the ball as soon as friends walk in the door! Things like having the tea and coffee all set up on a tray somewhere is really good. Coffee in the pot, tea leaves in the teapot, cups, sugar, teaspoons, milk in a jug, chocolates in a bowl. Just boil the kettle and pour. Also, flowers are a great distraction from the mess!

@kate_mckay_ceramics
@collector_wines

Spicy NUTTY SNACKING MIX
SPICED CAULIFLOWER *and* POTATOES
LAMB ROGAN JOSH *with baked rice, pickled onions and raita*
ROTI *with* CURRY SAUCE *and pickled cucumbers*
DESSERT BOXES

Everyone loves a curry, and this menu is such an easy way to feed four or eight or even twelve.

Spicy NUTTY SNACKING MIX

This spicy, nutty mix is great with drinks, but I also love it sprinkled over Spiced cauliflower and potatoes (right) or the Winter sun soup on page 198. I make ours quite spicy, but please adjust it to taste.

MAKES ABOUT 2 CUPS
PREP TIME : 10 MINS ❧ COOK TIME : 20 MINS

1 Tbsp vegetable oil
1 cup (150 g) raw cashews
1/3 cup (55 g) pepitas (pumpkin seeds)
1/3 cup (55 g) sunflower seeds
1 tsp honey
1 cup (200 g) tinned chickpeas, drained and rinsed

Spice mix
2 Tbsp garam masala
1 tsp salt
1 tsp ground turmeric
A pinch of chilli flakes, or to taste

Preheat the oven to 180°C (350°F).

To make the spice mix, place everything in a little jar and shake to combine.

Combine the oil, cashews, seeds, honey, chickpeas and spice mix in a bowl. Spread the mixture over a couple of baking trays. Pop the trays into the oven for 10 minutes, then give everything a good toss.

Return the trays to the oven for another 10 minutes or until the nuts and chickpeas look golden and the chickpeas are crispy. Set aside to cool completely, then store in a glass jar.

SPICED CAULIFLOWER _and_ POTATOES

This is such a handy and delicious recipe, and is great here as a side dish but also just beautiful served on its own as the main with a raita and roti or any flatbread to soak everything up. It's really good at room temperature so another option is to take it to a picnic or barbecue when you're asked to bring something and want to posh it up a bit without having to go to too much effort!

SERVES 6–8
PREP TIME : 15 MINS ❧ COOK TIME : 1 HOUR

1 cauliflower, cut into florets
750 g (1 lb 10 oz) potatoes, peeled and
   cut into wedges
1/3 cup (80 ml) olive oil
3 red onions, thinly sliced
2 garlic cloves, finely chopped
4 cm (1 1/2 inch) piece ginger, peeled and finely chopped
1 tsp ground cumin
1 tsp ground coriander
1 tsp ground turmeric
1/2 teaspoon fennel seeds
1 tsp sea salt
Spicy nutty snacking mix (see left), to serve (optional)
Chopped red chilli, to serve
Lime wedges, to serve

Preheat the oven to 180°C (350°F). Combine the cauliflower and potato on a baking tray, drizzle with half the olive oil and bake for about 40 minutes or until golden and the potatoes are cooked through.

Meanwhile, heat the remaining olive oil in a frying pan over low heat. Cook the onion for 10 minutes or until completely soft and caramelised. Stir in the garlic, ginger, cumin, coriander, turmeric, fennel seeds and salt and cook for a further 5 minutes.

Toss the spiced onion mixture with the potato and cauliflower and return to the oven for 20 minutes.

Sprinkle the potato and cauliflower with the nutty snacking mix, if using, and chilli. Serve with lime wedges and roti (see page 213) or other flatbread.

LAMB ROGAN JOSH

This gem of a curry is bursting with flavour and the perfect thing for a long wintery meal with friends. Plus (and here's another reason I love curries so much) it's prepared well in advance so all you need to do on the day is heat and gather.

The spice mix makes about double what you actually need for this recipe, but it's so useful that it's worth making extra for later. Use it to pep up a simple pumpkin soup, sprinkle over veggies before roasting and as a spice base for all kinds of braises, like the osso buco on page 188.

SERVES 8–10
PREP TIME : 20 MINS, PLUS OVERNIGHT MARINATING 〉 COOK TIME : ABOUT 4 HOURS

1.8–2 kg (4–4$\frac{1}{2}$ lb) lamb shoulder, diced
2 Tbsp ghee or olive oil
2 brown onions, thinly sliced
5 garlic cloves, thinly sliced
A good pinch of salt
2 bay leaves
2 Tbsp tomato paste (concentrated purée)
800 g (1 lb 12 oz) tin whole peeled tomatoes
Baked rice (see right), to serve
Chopped red chilli, to serve

Marinade
1 cup (260 g) Greek-style yoghurt
5 cm (2 inch) piece ginger, grated
5 garlic cloves, finely chopped
1 tsp ground turmeric

Spice mix
3 cinnamon sticks
50 g (1$\frac{3}{4}$ oz) yellow mustard seeds
50 g (1$\frac{3}{4}$ oz) cardamom pods
50 g (1$\frac{3}{4}$ oz) cumin seeds
25 g (1$\frac{3}{4}$ oz) fennel seeds
3 star anise

The day before you're going to serve the curry, combine the marinade ingredients in a bowl. Add the lamb and toss to coat. Cover and place in the fridge overnight or for at least 2 hours.

For the spice mix, combine all the ingredients in a dry frying pan. Stir over medium–high heat for 5 minutes or until the spices are aromatic and the seeds begin to pop. Transfer the mixture to a spice grinder, coffee grinder, high-powered blender or a mortar and pestle and blitz or bash until you have a fine powder.

At least 4 hours before lunch or dinner time, preheat the oven to 140°C (275°F). Place a large flameproof casserole dish over medium heat. Add the ghee or oil and cook the onion for about 10 minutes or until soft and translucent. Add the garlic and 3 tablespoons of the spice mix and cook for another few minutes, then stir in $\frac{1}{4}$ cup (60 ml) water.

Add the marinated lamb and salt and increase the heat to high. Cook, stirring well so the spiced onion mixture covers every piece of lamb, for 5 minutes. Reduce the heat to medium–low and stir in the bay leaves, tomato paste and tinned tomatoes.

At this point you can transfer the lamb mixture to a slow cooker and cook until the meat is nice and tender – I've cooked it on low all day and it's beautiful. Or, you could cover the dish and put it in the oven for 3–4 hours.

Serve the curry with rice, fresh chilli, pickled onions, raita and roti (page 213) or naan bread.

Baked rice

Preheat the oven to 160°C (320°F). Place 2 cups (400 g) basmati rice in an ovenproof dish and dot with 2 Tbsp (40 g) butter. Add some grated lemon zest, bay leaves and any other aromatics you like (a cinnamon stick would be lovely). Pour in boiling water to come about 1.5 cm (⁵⁄₈ inch) above the rice. Tightly cover the dish with foil and pop into the oven for about 40 minutes or until the rice is fluffy and all the water has been absorbed. *Serves 6–8*

Pickled onions

Thinly slice 3 large red onions and place them in a large jar. Combine 2 Tbsp salt, ¼ cup (55 g) sugar and 2 cups (500 ml) apple cider vinegar in a small saucepan. Place over medium heat and cook until just simmering, then continue cooking for a couple of minutes, whisking as you go. Remove the pan from the heat and pour the liquid over the onion. Pop the lid on the jar and leave to cool, then store the pickled onions in the fridge for up to 2 weeks. *Makes 1 large jar*

Raita

Roughly chop 1 handful coriander (cilantro) leaves and 1 handful mint leaves. Combine the herbs with the juice of 1 lemon, 1 Tbsp toasted sesame seeds, 1 Tbsp nigella seeds and ½ cup (130 g) Greek-style yoghurt. *Serves 6–8*

ROTI *with* CURRY SAUCE
and pickled cucumbers

*This one is for my husband Tim, who would happily have roti and curry sauce every night.
The roti are really easy and quite fun to make, and you can do so well in advance if that's
easier, then reheat them in a low oven. But actually, if the dough balls are all made, it's
quite fun to get your buddies or kids involved in the stretching and folding, then all you
need to do is quickly pan-fry the roti, one at a time.*

*And the curry sauce? It's just the easiest and most flavoursome condiment ever. I love to
make it into a quick noodle soup or pour it over rice and top it with a handful of steamed
greens for a quick dinner. It's also fabulous drizzled over a whole roasted cauliflower.*

SERVES 6–8
PREP TIME : 30 MINS, PLUS RESTING ⟩ COOK TIME : 50 MINS

3¹/2 cups (525 g) plain (all-purpose) flour
1 egg, at room temperature
2 Tbsp (40 g) butter, melted, plus softened
  butter for greasing
1 Tbsp sugar
1 tsp salt
Crunchy, tangy cucumber salad (page 42),
  to serve

Curry sauce
1 Tbsp vegetable oil
2 Tbsp red curry paste
400 g (14 oz) tin coconut milk
1 tsp brown sugar
1 Tbsp fish sauce
A pinch of salt

Combine the flour, egg, melted butter, sugar and salt with 1¹/4 cups (310 ml) water in the
bowl of a stand mixer fitted with a dough hook or in a large bowl. Knead until shiny and
elastic, about 5 minutes. Turn the dough out onto a work surface and cut it into 10 even
pieces. Shape each piece into a ball, rub with softened butter and place in a buttered dish.
Cover and place in the fridge overnight or leave it on the bench for at least a few hours.

To make the curry sauce, heat the oil in a saucepan over medium heat. Add the curry paste
and cook, stirring, for a minute or so until aromatic. Stir in the coconut milk, brown sugar,
fish sauce and salt. Reduce the heat to low and simmer for 5 minutes. Taste and adjust the
seasoning. Thin out the sauce with a little water if you think it's too thick. Keep the sauce
warm while you cook the roti.

Preheat the oven to 140°C (275°F). Rub a little softened butter on your work surface.
Flatten one dough ball with the palm of your hand, then gently stretch it out on the work
surface until it's as thin as possible and about 30 x 40 cm (12 x 16 inches). Don't worry
if there's the odd tear – just patch it up. Now fold the dough into a square, about 20 cm
(8 inches), and set aside while you roll the remaining dough, stacking the squares as you go.

Melt a good knob of butter in a frying pan over medium–high heat. Add one roti and cook
for a couple of minutes on each side until golden. Transfer to a tray lined with foil and keep
warm in the oven while you cook the remaining roti. Just before serving, scrunch each roti
in your hands a bit to roughen and fluff them up.

Serve the roti and curry sauce warm, with a little bowl of cucumber salad on the side.

DESSERT BOXES

The enthusiastic response you'll get from this 'dessert' will, I promise, be disproportionate to the amount of effort you've put into making it. Surprise and delight is what we are going for here, and you can't really lose when you make someone (of any age) a cute little box with their name on it, fill it with treats and present it to them for dessert.

Find some little cardboard boxes from the craft section of your local discount shop (or just wrap your treats in napkins tied with ribbon), add some name tags and hide them until dessert.

Ideas for treats for dessert boxes

- Assorted sweets and chocolates

- Chocolate-covered fruit and nut mix (great for little competitions – if you bite into a nut, you need to sing a line from your favourite song; if you bite into a fruity chocolate, you need to recite a stanza of a favourite poem or tell a joke)

- A little conversation starter (see page 218) or trivia question on a scrap of paper

- A tiny toy or brooch

- Caramel popcorn (store-bought, or use the recipe on page 218)

- Chocolate truffles (store-bought, or use the Praline truffle recipe on page 80)

- A few strawberries and/or raspberries

On being good company

I am very far from being any expert on etiquette, but I do know from experience that there are some gestures that are always appreciated. Here is my 'crash course' on being good company.

1. **Don't arrive on time!** Never, ever, ever knock on that door until 10 minutes after the advertised start time.

2. **Sing for your supper.** I have a lovely friend from school days who epitomises this. Every time she is invited to a friend's house she is on form – she tells funny and appropriate stories, and she is enthusiastic, curious and fun to be around. Once I asked her why she puts such an effort into being a good guest and she told me her mum drilled into her from a young age that you must always 'sing for your supper'. I love that!

3. **Be generous with the booze and bring it cold.** It's always nice to bring an extra bottle of wine, sparkling water or beer – something to share on the night and a bottle for your hosts to have later while thinking nice things about you. And if you're bringing beer or chilled wine, score bonus consideration points by bringing it in a cooler bag with an ice brick so that your friend doesn't have to make room in their overcrowded fridge for your six-pack.

4. **Know when to leave.** There's always a natural end to any gathering. It's a bit of an art to catch that point and begin the leaving process so your hosts aren't politely making conversation with you at 1am on a school night when they're desperate to go to bed. Don't have one for the road... get on the road!

5. **Bring a little 'thank you' gift.** Ideally this should be something that doesn't need to be dealt with anytime soon, so your host can just say 'thank you so much', pop it on the counter and come back to it later. The recipes on the following pages are perfect for such a gift.

More ideas for 'thank you' gifts

- A bag of Walnut and fennel biscotti (page 151)
- A little bunch of herbs from your garden
- A little jar of Simple dukkah (page 99) or Sweet dukkah (page 161)
- A jar of Rhubarb, orange and pistachio thumbprint cookies (page 157)
- A box of Praline truffles (page 80)

CARAMEL POPCORN *with smashed pretzels*
CONVERSATION-STARTER COOKIES
MANDARIN *and* VANILLA SUGAR ❧ MANDARIN *and* FENNEL SALT
Ali's TOASTED COCONUT MARSHMALLOWS
BLOOD ORANGE SHRUB ❧ ORANGE SHERBET

All of these recipes make a perfect little 'thank you' gift for your hosts.

CARAMEL POPCORN
with smashed pretzels

I would be thrilled if someone brought over a little jar or bag of this crunchy, sweet, salty and addictive snack any time. (Hint, hint!)

MAKES ABOUT 5 CUPS
PREP TIME : 10 MINS } COOK TIME : 25 MINS

5 cups (100 g) popped popcorn
1 cup (220 g) firmly packed brown sugar
150 g (5^{1}/$_{2}$ oz) butter
^{1}/$_{2}$ cup (150 g) liquid glucose
1 tsp vanilla bean paste
1 tsp sea salt
2 cups (90 g) pretzels, gently smashed

Preheat the oven to 160°C (320°F). Spread the popcorn over two lined baking trays.

Combine the sugar, butter and liquid glucose in a saucepan. Cook over medium heat until the mixture reaches 115°C (239°F) on a sugar thermometer. Remove from the heat and stir in the vanilla and salt. Pour the caramel over the popcorn and stir to coat. Bake for 20 minutes, stirring after 10 minutes. Set aside to cool completely.

Break up the popcorn and combine it with the smashed pretzels. Store the mixture in jars.

Ideas for 'conversation starters'

- What is your karaoke song?
- What's the best birthday present you've ever received?
- What book has influenced you most?
- What's the song that always gets you dancing?
- What talent do you wish you had?
- Name the three things you'd take if you were going to be stuck on a desert island.

CONVERSATION-STARTER COOKIES

These cookies are great to bring out after dinner. You'll need some 'conversation starters' on strips of paper. It's fun to tailor them to your fellow diners.

MAKES 10–15
PREP TIME : 30 MINS } COOK TIME : ABOUT 45 MINS

Vegetable oil, for greasing
^{1}/$_{2}$ cup (110 g) sugar
^{1}/$_{2}$ cup (75 g) plain (all-purpose) flour
A pinch of salt
2 egg whites
^{1}/$_{2}$ tsp vanilla extract
A couple of drops of almond essence (optional)
Conversation starters (see below left for ideas)

Preheat the oven to 200°C (400°F). Grease a baking sheet with vegetable oil and grease a large offset spatula or flat knife. Have a muffin tin ready for cooling the cookies.

Whisk the sugar, flour and salt in a bowl.

Whisk the egg whites and vanilla together. Pour the mixture into the dry ingredients with the almond essence, if using, and whisk until smooth.

Place a spoonful of batter on the baking sheet and, using the greased spatula or knife, gently spread it out to a 7 cm (2^{3}/$_{4}$ inch) circle. It doesn't have to be perfect, but ensure it's fairly even. Repeat to make a second circle. Bake the cookies for 5–6 minutes or until the edges are golden brown.

Remove the tray from the oven and, working quickly, flip each cookie over and place a conversation starter in the middle of each one. Fold each cookie in half like a taco and press the edges together, then fold in half again to create a 'bent elbow' fortune cookie shape. Place the cookies in the muffin tin so they hold their shape as they cool and crisp up. Repeat until all the batter has been used.

Store the cooled cookies in an airtight container for a week or so.

MANDARIN *and* VANILLA SUGAR

This little condiment is so beautiful in so many applications and makes a great gift when visiting friends as it doesn't need to be kept in the fridge. It lasts for a while and is absolutely delicious.

MAKES ABOUT 1 CUP
PREP TIME : 10 MINS ❱ COOK TIME : 3 HOURS

4 mandarins (unsprayed/organic/homegrown,
  if possible)
1 vanilla bean, split lengthways
1 cup (220 g) golden caster (superfine) sugar

Peel the mandarins, pulling away as much of the white pith as possible. Place the peel on a baking tray and pop it in the lowest possible oven for a few hours – I had mine at 70°C (150°F). Alternatively, leave it near the fireplace or out in the sun for a few days. Basically, you want the peel to be as dry as possible.

Transfer the dried peel to a blender, spice grinder or mortar and pestle and blitz or bash until it forms a coarse powder (it will make about 3 teaspoons).

Scrape the vanilla seeds into a bowl with the sugar and the ground mandarin peel. Mix well with your fingertips, rubbing the mandarin peel and vanilla seeds into the sugar. Store the sugar in a jar.

Uses for mandarin and vanilla sugar

- Sprinkle it over a hot chocolate or chocolate mousse for a lovely jaffa situation.
- Use it in baking – substitute the sugar with some or all of this flavoured sugar.
- Sprinkle it over the top of shortbread biscuits before baking.
- Sprinkle it over some rhubarb pieces and squeeze a little mandarin or orange juice over the top, then roast until tender.

MANDARIN *and* FENNEL SALT

Make up a few jars of this salt and keep them on hand for quick gifts. I love having an 'edible present drawer' full of things like this, little jars of jam or other long-lasting goodies.

MAKES ABOUT 1 CUP
PREP TIME : 5 MINS ❱ COOK TIME : 5 MINS

3 tsp fennel seeds
3 tsp ground mandarin peel (see Mandarin and
  vanilla sugar, left)
1 cup (130 g) sea salt flakes

Toast the fennel seeds in a dry frying pan. Transfer to a small bowl to cool.

Add the ground mandarin peel and sea salt to the fennel and mix well with your fingertips, rubbing the mandarin peel into the salt. Adjust to taste, adding more mandarin peel or salt if needed. Store the salt in a jar.

Uses for mandarin and fennel salt

- Sprinkle it over a really simple soup, such as cauliflower, for a jolt of extra flavour.
- Sprinkle it over fish before (or after) pan-frying.
- Sprinkle it over chicken before roasting.
- Sprinkle it over vegetables before roasting.

Recipes pictured page 223

Ali's TOASTED COCONUT MARSHMALLOWS

I met Ali in mothers' group 12 years ago and she's been bringing these marshmallows to gatherings ever since. I'm very grateful to her for sharing the recipe. It makes loads of marshmallows, but they last for ages and are lovely gifts.

MAKES ABOUT 40
PREP TIME : 20 MINS, PLUS SETTING
COOK TIME : 30 MINUTES

1/3 cup (60 g) powdered gelatine
4 cups (880 g) caster (superfine) sugar
2 cups (500 ml) boiling water
Finely grated zest of 1 lemon
2 tsp lemon juice
2 tsp vanilla extract
2 cups (130 g) desiccated coconut, toasted

Combine the gelatine and 1 cup (250 ml) cold water in a small jug. Set aside.

Place the sugar and boiling water in a large saucepan. Cook over low heat, stirring often, until the sugar has dissolved. Bring to the boil, add the gelatine mixture and whisk to combine. Reduce the heat and simmer for 20 minutes.

Transfer the mixture to the bowl of an electric mixer fitted with the whisk attachment. Set aside to cool for 20 minutes.

Add the lemon zest, lemon juice and vanilla to the gelatine mixture and beat for a good 10 minutes or until the mixture is very thick and white. When it's almost ready, rinse two 20 cm (8 inch) square cake tins with water, but don't dry them. Divide the marshmallow mixture between the tins and refrigerate until set, about 30 minutes.

Put the coconut in a bowl. Cut the marshmallow into squares with a wet knife. Lift out the squares with a spatula and then toss them in the coconut, pressing down so the marshmallows are covered. Store in an airtight container for up to 2 weeks.

BLOOD ORANGE SHRUB

Use the shrub in salad dressings or as a cordial mixed with mineral water and ice. It's especially good added to a simple gin and tonic.

MAKES ABOUT 4 CUPS (1 LITRE)
PREP TIME : 10 MINS } COOK TIME : NIL

4 blood oranges
About 1 cup (250 ml) white balsamic vinegar
About 1 cup (220 g) caster (superfine) sugar

Peel the oranges, reserving the peel, then squeeze the oranges with your hands to extract as much juice as possible. Weigh the juice into a bowl and add the same weight of vinegar and sugar. Whisk well. Pack the peel into a jar and pour in the juice mixture. Seal and shake well. Store in the fridge for up to a week.

ORANGE SHERBET

This sherbet is beautiful with lots of mineral water and ice, or mixed into a tangy cocktail – lovely with vermouth or just a splash of vodka.

MAKES ABOUT 4 CUPS (1 LITRE)
PREP TIME : 5 MINS, PLUS STANDING
COOK TIME : NIL

4 large oranges
About 1 cup (220 g) caster (superfine) sugar

Peel the oranges and place the peel in a bowl, then squeeze the oranges with your hands to extract as much juice as possible. Weigh the juice and add the same weight of sugar to the bowl with the orange peel. Keep the juice in the fridge until needed.

Massage the sugar and peel together, then transfer to a jar and shake well. Set aside in a cool place for 4 hours, shaking occasionally. Pour the orange juice into the jar and shake well, then strain away the peel. Store the sherbet in the fridge for up to 2 weeks.

Wintery ploughman's lunch

We are so lucky here in Orange to be surrounded not only by beautiful orchards and vineyards, but also friends who make and share wine from the latter and share the former with us for apple picking and picnics. The Swift family of Printhie Wines have a long tradition of making some of this region's finest wines and they also happen to be good friends to us. It was such a pleasure to share an afternoon with them in the golden, early winter sunshine and graze on a ploughman's lunch with an apple pie and a few bottles of Printhie's best wine.

I don't think there is anything more lovely or picnic-perfect than a good ploughman's lunch. Add a lamb chop straight off the grill and you have, perhaps, my ultimate meal.

Em Swift's notes on wine and picnics

Picnics and wine are the perfect partners, but it's best to keep your wine selection to varieties that will go with lots of different dishes, especially if your guests are all bringing food along. For picnics on those long warm afternoons, consider a pinot gris followed by rosé. If picnicking during the cooler months, warm yourselves up with a pinot meunier and then cabernet, which goes perfectly with cheese platters. Sparkling is a must to start – no matter what time of year it is! (And note that a pressure stopper is the best way to keep opened sparkling wine fresh for several days. Please do not use a spoon in the bottle – that is a complete myth!)

Pairing food and wine

- White meat generally goes with white wine.
- Spicy food suits pinot gris, riesling and rosé.
- Red meat can take the heavier reds – lamb with cabernet and beef with shiraz.
- Game meat such as duck and venison goes very well with pinot noir or pinot meunier.
- Sparkling (preferably *méthode traditionnelle*) goes well with seafood and lighter-flavoured menus.

@printhiewines

Big *flavour* TOMATO SOUP
PLOUGHMAN'S *with a chop and* BEETROOT PICKLED EGGS
Narnie's APPLE PIE
CHOCOLATE, CARAMEL *and* TOASTED SESAME SLICE

I don't think there is anything more lovely or picnic-perfect than a good ploughman's lunch.

Big flavour
TOMATO SOUP

A little mug of this soup by a bonfire or fire pit, or at the kitchen table, delivers big, bright flavours and comfort. Best of all, it uses pretty much all pantry ingredients, so it would also be a perfect contender for my 'Loaves and fishes' repertoire of recipes on page 184. Keep the soup hot in a big thermos and pour it into little cups to warm hands and tummies at a wintery picnic. My kids also love this with toast soldiers for dinner.

You can roast and peel the capsicums yourself or just buy a jar of roasted capsicums that are all ready to go.

SERVES 8–10 AS A STARTER
PREP TIME : 15 MINS ⟩ COOK TIME : 45 MINS

1/3 cup (80 ml) olive oil
1 brown onion, roughly chopped
2 roasted red capsicums (peppers), halved,
   seeded and roughly chopped
4 garlic cloves, roughly chopped
2 Tbsp thyme leaves
1/4 cup (60 g) tomato paste (concentrated purée)
800 g (1 lb 12 oz) tin whole peeled tomatoes
2 cups (500 ml) chicken or vegetable stock
1 tsp red wine vinegar
A sprinkle of Simple dukkah (page 99), to serve

Heat the olive oil in a large saucepan over medium heat. Cook the onion for about 5 minutes or until translucent. Add the capsicum, garlic and thyme and cook, stirring often, for another 5 minutes.

Add the tomato paste, tinned tomatoes, stock and red wine vinegar and season with salt and pepper. Stir well and bring to the boil, then reduce the heat and simmer for about 30 minutes. Remove from the heat and cool slightly.

Transfer the soup to a blender and blitz until smooth. Check the flavour to balance the acidity of the tomatoes, and perhaps add a little more salt.

Serve the soup sprinkled with a little dukkah for extra flavour and crunch.

PLOUGHMAN'S
with a chop

Imagine spending a bright, clear winter's day sitting outside on a picnic rug, enjoying a ploughman's lunch with a lamb chop straight off the barbecue – now that's one of the most pleasant picnics you'll ever have!

A ploughman's lunch is, like any simple meal of good ingredients, greater than the sum of its parts: a crunchy apple, a sharp hunk of cheddar, some good bread, pickles and plenty of sunshine. What could be nicer? This is a great way to feed just yourself, small groups or even a bunch of people at a party, in which case I'd recommend buying and glazing a whole ham as well.

Here are the basic elements of a really great ploughman's lunch, but you can add or remove ingredients to taste:

· Cheddar cheese

· Good-quality ham

· Really good, crispy, crunchy apples

· Beetroot pickled eggs (page 229)

· Bread and butter pickles, kraut or any pickles you have lurking around in the fridge

· Sliced, crusty bread

· Tomato (or other) relish

· Grainy mustard.

BEETROOT PICKLED EGGS

So pretty. So retro. And so good (trust me). I do understand that the idea of pickled eggs might sound a bit unusual, but actually they are quite delicious and perfect in a ploughman's lunch, topped with salty capers.

SERVES 8–10 AS PART OF A PLOUGHMAN'S PLATTER
PREP TIME : 15 MINS, PLUS 1–3 DAYS STANDING ⟩ COOK TIME : 15 MINS

5 eggs
1 tsp fennel seeds
6 juniper berries
6 black peppercorns
6 pink peppercorns
1 cup (250 ml) red wine vinegar
2 bay leaves
1/2 cup (110 g) sugar
2 beetroot, quartered

Cook the eggs in a saucepan of boiling water for about 6–7 minutes (up to 10 minutes if you want them really hard-boiled). Drain the eggs and plunge them into cold water to stop them cooking. Peel and set aside.

Clean and dry the saucepan, then add the fennel seeds, juniper berries and peppercorns and toast for 5 minutes or until aromatic. Pour in the vinegar and 1 cup (250 ml) water. Add the bay leaves, sugar and beetroot. Bring to the boil, stirring to dissolve the sugar. Remove from the heat and set aside to cool.

Put the eggs in the bottom of a large sterilised jar and pour in enough of the pickling mixture to ensure the eggs are completely submerged. Seal the top with a round of baking paper and put the lid on the jar. Leave in a cool, dark place for 1–3 days.

Discard the beetroot and store the eggs and pickling liquid in the fridge for up to 2 weeks.

NOTE
I sterilise my jars by washing them in a hot dishwasher, then heating them in a 180°C (350°F) oven for 15 minutes.

NARNIE'S APPLE PIE

This is, without a doubt, the best apple pie I have ever tasted. It comes via my friend Amber, whose husband Derek took the mantle of making it for every family gathering soon after he joined her family. This recipe is exactly what this book is about: families and friends coming together over food, creating traditions and taking the time to cook delicious things for each other. Thank you to Derek and the pie's original creator, Dot Ryan, for sharing the recipe.

SERVES 8-10
PREP TIME : 30 MINS ⅜ COOK TIME : 40 MINS

12 tart Granny Smith apples, peeled, cored
   and sliced
3/4 cup (165 g) caster (superfine) sugar
4 cloves

Pastry
1 cup (250 g) unsalted butter, softened
1/2 cup (110 g) caster (superfine) sugar,
   plus extra for sprinkling
1 large egg, plus 1 egg, extra, for brushing
1 tsp vanilla extract
1 cup (150 g) plain (all-purpose) flour
1/2 cup (75 g) self-raising flour

Combine the apple, sugar, cloves and 1/2 cup (125 ml) water in a large saucepan. Cook over medium–low heat for 10 minutes or until the apple is soft (don't overcook it or it will be too watery). Dig out the cloves and set the pan aside. Preheat the oven to 200°C (400°F).

For the pastry, put the butter in the bowl of an electric mixer fitted with the whisk attachment and beat until pale and fluffy. Add the sugar and beat until the mixture has doubled in volume, at least 6 minutes. Add the egg and vanilla and beat until well combined. Change to the paddle attachment and reduce the mixer speed. Add the flour, 1 tablespoon at a time. Once all the flour has been added, the dough should be quite stiff and dry.

Place two-thirds of the pastry in a 24 cm (9½ inch) spring-form tin. Gently push the pastry out to cover the base and come about 3 cm (1¼ inches) up the side, as evenly as possible. Don't worry if it looks a bit lumpy – it will puff up on cooking and will be quite fluffy.

Return the saucepan of apple to the stovetop and bring to the boil (you want it to be really hot when it hits the pastry as this cooks the base and side). Gently spoon the hot apple into the pie shell.

Take small pieces of the remaining pastry and crumble it over the apple, covering as much of the apple as possible. (Keep in mind that the pastry will puff and expand as it cooks, so it should form itself into a fairly cohesive pie topping in the oven.)

Whisk the extra egg and brush it over the pie, then sprinkle it with the extra sugar. Bake for 30 minutes or until the pie is golden. Watch carefully towards the end – you might need to reduce the heat to 180°C (350°F) if the pastry is cooking too quickly.

The pie should be golden and a thing of beauty when you take it out of the oven. But please don't attempt to cut it straight away or everything will collapse into a crumbly (albeit delicious) mess. Leave it to cool and firm up in the tin, then cut it once it's at room temperature or even from the fridge. Reheat the pie if you like, but I love it best cold.

CHOCOLATE, CARAMEL *and* TOASTED SESAME SLICE

My daughter Alice said that this was the best thing I've ever made. I took her praise gladly, but also in the pragmatic knowledge that a slice like this is always going to be a big hit. How could it not be, with those layers of shortbread, caramel and chocolate? And this one is extra good with the toasted sesame seeds in the base and sprinkled on top.

A word of warning: this slice is very, very rich, so cut it into small squares and perhaps give any leftovers to the neighbours to stop yourself from sneaking a piece here and there and then feeling a little bit ill (I write from experience).

MAKES ABOUT 25 PIECES
PREP TIME : 25 MINS, PLUS CHILLING 》 COOK TIME : 40 MINS

Shortbread base
1/2 cup (125 g) chilled unsalted butter,
   cut into cubes
3/4 cup (110 g) plain (all-purpose) flour
2/3 cup (85 g) icing (confectioners') sugar
1/3 cup (50 g) toasted sesame seeds
A pinch of salt

Caramel layer
2 x 400 g (14 oz) tins sweetened
   condensed milk
1/3 cup (80 g) butter
1/3 cup (115 g) golden syrup

Chocolate topping
2 cups (300 g) chopped chocolate
   (dark or milk – whatever you prefer)
1 tsp coconut oil or vegetable oil
Toasted sesame seeds and sea salt flakes,
   for sprinkling

Preheat the oven to 180°C (350°F). Grease a 25 cm (10 inch) square slice tin and line the tin with baking paper.

For the base, combine all the ingredients in a food processor and blitz until the mixture looks like coarse sand and holds together when you squeeze it. Press into the tin and use the back of a spoon to smooth it into an even layer. Bake for 20 minutes or until the base is pale gold. Remove from the oven and let it cool for at least 5 minutes before adding the caramel.

While the base is cooking, make the caramel layer. Combine the condensed milk, butter and golden syrup in a saucepan. Cook over medium–low heat, stirring often, for 10 minutes or until the ingredients have melted together and you have a thick, golden caramel. Pour the caramel over the shortbread base and bake for 20 minutes. Remove from the oven and leave to cool for 10 minutes, then pop it into the fridge to cool completely.

Melt the chocolate in a heatproof glass bowl over a saucepan of simmering water. Stir in the oil, then pour the mixture over the caramel layer and smooth the top. Sprinkle the sesame seeds and sea salt over the chocolate. Place in the fridge for 2 hours or until completely set.

Cut the slice into squares using a serrated knife (or you'll risk squashing the layers together!) and store in a cool place.

Filling the hollow legs

As my kids enter their teenage years, I have been turning to friends with older teens and parenting podcasts to arm me with tips to navigate what I'm sure will be an interesting period. And here's what really stuck: we want our kids to bring their friends home as much as possible, so we get to know who they are hanging out with and know they're safe and under our roof. To encourage this, one recommendation is to make sure you are well stocked with snacks and food they'll love.

Well, I might stumble and fall on many parenting fronts, but rustling up yummy food? That I can do!

My tips for filling those 'hollow legs' that never seem to get full

- Overcater! Teenagers always seem to hoover up more than you think they will, so be extra generous, especially with the chicken wings – they disappear very quickly.
- Home-made popcorn with sea salt is a fantastic snack to put out at the beginning of the party, as is a big plate of chopped, crunchy vegetables, corn chips and a big bowl of hummus.
- Involve your kids in the catering, from choosing what to cook to preparing the food.
- When it comes to drinks, I'm not a huge fan of soft drinks so I try to avoid buying them, but I find that a big portable water cooler mixed with lemon or orange cordial does the trick on a picnic. At home, I use our beloved SodaStream to make up jugs of fizzy lemon juice (lemon cordial with sparkling water), with lots of ice, some mint leaves and maybe even a few raspberries or chopped strawberries if I want to be extra fancy.
- Portability is key – go for food that can be held and eaten in one hand and on the move, because good luck getting everyone to stay put to eat! That's why hamburgers are so good, as are chicken wings, wraps, sausage rolls, sushi and pizza.
- Another all-time winner when you have a big group to feed (of any age!) is to serve a big glazed ham, surrounded with lots of bread rolls, a few mustards and maybe a slaw. The porchetta on page 16 would be similarly popular.
- I find that if I set up food in 'stations' (as per the meringue sundaes on page 240) and go to even a tiny bit of effort to make it look special, the kids do appreciate it and love making up their own creations.

Sticky spiced CHICKEN WINGS
HAMBURGERS *with miso butter and pink sauce*
BROWN SUGAR MERINGUE SUNDAES

This menu is a proven winner with all kinds of small, medium-sized and fully grown humans, but especially teens.

Sticky spiced CHICKEN WINGS

These are always a big hit – so much flavour and colour and goodness, and so easy to throw together. Plus, they smell amazing while they're cooking. You can also turn this into a meal in itself by roasting some sweet potato wedges and perhaps some broccoli florets with the chicken wings. Add some cooked pearl couscous to the tray as it comes out, then toss everything together.

SERVES 6 (AS A STARTER)
PREP TIME : 10 MINS, PLUS MARINATING ⟩ COOK TIME : 1 HOUR

1 kg (2 lb 4 oz) chicken wings
1/4 cup (60 ml) olive oil
1 Tbsp brown sugar
1/2 tsp chilli flakes
2 tsp smoked paprika
1/2 tsp ground cumin
1 tsp sea salt
Grated zest and juice of 1 lime

Lime dipping sauce
1/2 cup (130 g) Greek-style yoghurt
1 handful coriander (cilantro) leaves, roughly
    chopped
Grated zest and juice of 1 lime

Put the chicken wings, olive oil, brown sugar, spices, sea salt, lime zest and juice in a large container with a lid. Massage the marinade into the chicken wings, then cover and marinate in the fridge for at least 1 hour or overnight.

Preheat the oven to 180°C (350°F). Tip the chicken wings and marinade into a roasting tin and cook for 1 hour or until the chicken is cooked through and golden brown.

Meanwhile, for the lime dipping sauce, mix the yoghurt with the coriander, lime zest and lime juice and season to taste.

Serve the hot chicken wings with the dipping sauce.

HAMBURGERS
with miso butter and pink sauce

These burgers are always a crowd-pleaser and an easy way to feed a hungry horde. The idea for doing burgers this way comes via Tara O'Brady's excellent book, Seven Spoons (I just love her food writing and cooking). The miso butter is perfect on these burgers, but also on countless other things. I highly recommend doubling the recipe as it's fabulous in a baked potato, spread over salmon before baking, or tossed through steamed broccoli, and so on.

The pink sauce is nothing fancy but it's completely delicious – it's a nod to the 'pink sauce' made famous by a school friend's dad. Whenever she brought friends home for the weekend, he'd make burgers and serve them with this sauce. I loved it so much.

SERVES 6
PREP TIME : 20 MINS 〉 COOK TIME : 5 MINS

600 g (1 lb 5 oz) beef mince
6 brioche burger buns
6 slices gruyere or other soft, melty cheese
Bread and butter pickles, to serve
1 handful curly endive or other lettuce

Miso butter
1/3 cup (80 g) butter, softened
1 Tbsp white miso
Grated zest of 1 lime

Pink sauce
1/2 cup (120 g) mayonnaise
1/4 cup (30 g) bread and butter pickles,
   finely chopped
2 Tbsp tomato sauce
1 Tbsp dijon mustard
1/4 tsp smoked paprika

Start by making the miso butter. Mix the butter with the miso and lime zest until well combined. Shape the butter into a log, roll it in baking paper and pop it into the fridge or keep it at room temperature if you're using it straight away.

For the pink sauce, combine all the ingredients in a jug and whisk together. Check the seasoning and adjust to taste.

Season the beef with salt and pepper, then shape it into 6 patties, about 10 cm (4 inches) wide and 2 cm (3/4 inch) thick (they will shrink as they cook, so make them a little wider than the bun bases). Place the patties on a tray, tightly cover and pop them into the fridge until you're ready to cook.

Heat your barbecue or grill plate to high and preheat the oven to 180°C (350°F).

Warm the burger buns in the oven while you cook the patties for 3 minutes on each side (or until done to your liking).

Split open the warm burger buns and spread one side with the miso butter. Plonk the just-cooked patties down on the buns and top with the cheese, pickles, pink sauce and lettuce. Bombs away!

BROWN SUGAR MERINGUE SUNDAES

BROWN SUGAR MERINGUES
YOGHURT CREAM
CHOCOLATE FUDGE SAUCE
Home-made HONEYCOMB
Roasted hazelnuts

This is one of those desserts that always pleases. It feeds a crowd pretty easily (and affordably) and makes a fun alternative to a birthday cake for a kids' party (you can just stick a candle in one of the meringues).

I like to put everything out in jars so that people can decorate their own meringue or even smash it up into a jar or cup and make it a mess of goodness. You could also add some poached quince (page 175) or rhubarb (page 138) or pieces of blood orange, but when I suggested that to the boys they grimaced and told me that fruit would only ruin a perfectly good treat!

You could also make this up as a pavlova and top it with all the goodies.

Keeping in mind that the meringues and the honeycomb will both keep in airtight containers for a good 2 weeks, this is a great dessert for all of those super-organised people to prepare way in advance.

If you don't have loads of time, you could use nice store-bought ice cream here instead of the meringues, or even store-bought meringues and honeycomb to make this a super-quick dessert.

BROWN SUGAR MERINGUES

Using brown sugar as well as caster sugar gives these meringues a beautiful caramel-like look and flavour. You could also add some warm spices such as ground cinnamon, cloves and nutmeg to make them extra special, but I'm not sure my kids would love that little twist!

SERVES 6–8
PREP TIME : 15 MINS, PLUS COOLING
COOK TIME : 1 HOUR

6 large egg whites
A pinch of salt
3/4 cup (165 g) caster (superfine) sugar
2/3 cup (150 g) firmly packed brown sugar
1 tsp vanilla extract

Preheat the oven to 140°C (275°F). Line two baking trays with baking paper.

Put the egg whites and salt in the bowl of an electric mixer fitted with the whisk attachment and whisk until stiff peaks form.

Meanwhile, put the sugars in a bowl and whisk to combine. Add to the stiff egg whites, a tablespoon at a time, and keep whisking until all the sugar is incorporated into the meringue, then add the vanilla and continue beating for 2 minutes.

Using two tablespoons, spoon the meringue mixture onto the trays. Leave a few centimetres between each one.

Pop the trays into the oven for 5 minutes, then reduce the heat to 100°C (200°F). Bake for 1 hour. Turn off the oven and leave the meringues in there to cool for a few hours or even overnight.

Store the meringues in an airtight container for up to 2 weeks.

YOGHURT CREAM

Adding the yoghurt to the whipped cream seems to keep the cream from deflating if you are storing it in the fridge for a while (or transporting it in a cool box or insulated bag). It also cuts through some of the sweetness from the meringue, honeycomb and chocolate sauce.

SERVES 6–8
PREP TIME : 5 MINS } COOK TIME : NIL

1 cup (250 ml) single (pure) cream
1/2 cup (130 g) Greek-style yoghurt

Whip the cream until soft peaks form. Gently fold in the yoghurt and transfer to a jar or bowl. Store in the fridge until serving.

Recipes pictured pages 240–241

CHOCOLATE FUDGE SAUCE

Bring a jar of fudgy hot chocolate sauce to the table and you're instantly winning. This keeps for up to a week in the fridge and also makes a great little present for someone (see 'On being good company' on page 216).

MAKES ABOUT 2 CUPS (500 ML)
PREP TIME : 5 MINS   COOK TIME : 15 MINS

1 cup (250 ml) single (pure) cream
1/2 cup (110 g) firmly packed brown sugar
1 Tbsp (20 g) butter
11/2 cups (225 g) roughly chopped good-quality
    chocolate (I use half milk and half dark)
1 tsp vanilla bean paste

Combine the cream, brown sugar and butter in a saucepan. Stir over medium heat for a few minutes or until everything has melted into a lovely hot cream sauce. Bring just to boiling point, then remove from the heat and stir in the chocolate and the vanilla. Stir until the chocolate melts into the hot cream mixture and you have a smooth sauce.

Serve the sauce warm or keep it in the fridge and reheat it just before serving. (You can do this in the microwave, but we don't have one so I put the jar in a saucepan of boiling water and leave it for a few minutes, giving it a stir every now and then until the sauce softens and warms up.)

Home-made HONEYCOMB

I love making honeycomb and it really is pretty easy, but you could also buy plain honeycomb or the chocolate-covered version and smash that up.

MAKES 1 LARGE JAR
PREP TIME : 5 MINS   COOK TIME : 15 MINS

1 Tbsp bicarbonate of soda (baking soda)
1 cup (220 g) caster (superfine) sugar
1/3 cup (115 g) honey
2 Tbsp liquid glucose

Grease a deep-sided 20 x 30 cm (8 x 12 inch) roasting tin and line the tin with baking paper.

Spoon the bicarbonate of soda into a small bowl and whisk or mash with a spoon to get rid of any lumps. Set aside.

Combine the sugar, honey and liquid glucose with 2 tablespoons water in a large saucepan. Bring to the boil over medium–high heat, stirring, then cook for 5 minutes or until the mixture turns a golden caramel colour or reaches 160°C (320°F) on a sugar thermometer. Remove the pan from the heat.

Working quickly, sprinkle the bicarbonate of soda onto the hot caramel mixture and stir until just combined. Pour into the lined tin and set aside to cool and harden.

Break the honeycomb into shards and store it in an airtight container for up to 2 weeks or so.

Variation

My kids love it when I let some nice vanilla ice cream soften and stir through honeycomb shards, chocolate chips and frozen raspberries, then return it to the freezer to firm up.

Another cute idea is to freeze balls of this ice-cream mixture in muffin tins lined with paper cases, then dip the balls into melted chocolate and serve them as honeycomb bombs. It's a fun and easy treat to make for kids' parties.

Sunday best

This is probably the most grown-up menu in the book, but it's also one of the easiest. The eye fillet is a bit extravagant, I know, but every now and then it's nice to treat yourself with a really beautiful cut of meat. It's a great menu for a celebration lunch or dinner, when you want to impress or just spoil your favourite people with something special.

Instead of a big heavy pudding, shift gears for this wintery lunch from the main meal to a bright, fun jug of orange sherbet cocktails and pass around a plate of jewelled chocolate bark. Even better, get up from the table and head out to a fire pit or fireplace.

We shared this meal at The Repose, a lovely B&B in Dubbo, New South Wales, with its creators and co-owners, Jemima Aldridge (also of Saddler & Co.) and Moir Jones, who invited a few friends for a much-deserved long wintery lunch. Jemima and Moir took a small cottage just shy of the centre of town and over the space of 18 months (while also running separate businesses and big families), carefully transformed it into the most dreamy space. They've filled every corner with art, linen, candles and curiosities, making it the perfect place for a long weekend or just a leisurely lunch.

Jemima's tips for setting the scene when friends come over

A couple of personal touches is all that's needed to add a sense of occasion to the common dining table. I like to collect little pieces from candle makers, weavers and ceramic potters and use them with joy for special meals. I also create a design highlight by styling the table with a favourite antique piece, or a collection of interesting or unexpected objects. Gather seasonal foliage that's growing in your garden or on the side of the road. Try a cut branch of leaves and simply lay it on the table, which won't obstruct the flow of conversation. Only use ambient lighting to create a zone of comfort, and put on some music or unearth the old record player. With a little planning, the meal can be a lingering affair, where no-one wants to leave!

@the_repose
@jemima.aldridge
@saddlerandco

CARAMELISED FENNEL *and* BRIE DIP

WINTER GREENS *with garlic and almonds*

ROASTED EYE FILLET *with* QUINCE GLAZE
and parsnip and onion purée

CHOCOLATE BARK ❦ ORANGE SHERBET COCKTAILS

This is a great menu for a celebration lunch or dinner.

CARAMELISED FENNEL *and* BRIE DIP

Honestly, this warm cheesy dip is heaven, especially served with some chilled bubbles or a chardonnay at the beginning of the meal. You could swap the fennel with caramelised onions if you prefer, but as there are onions in the parsnip purée with the beef, I thought fennel might be good and it really is.

SERVES 4–6 AS A STARTER

PREP TIME : 10 MINS COOK TIME : 15 MINS

1/3 cup (80 ml) olive oil
2 fennel bulbs, thinly sliced, fronds reserved
1 Tbsp thyme leaves
400 g (14 oz) brie cheese, thinly sliced
1/2 cup (45 g) grated parmesan cheese
A pinch of chilli flakes

Heat the oil in a large frying pan over medium–high heat. Cook the fennel for 6 minutes or until soft and caramelised. Combine the caramelised fennel with the thyme, brie and parmesan in an ovenproof serving dish.

Just before serving, put the dish under a hot grill until the dip is bubbling and golden brown.

Sprinkle the chilli flakes over the dip and serve it with radicchio leaves and lavosh crackers or toasted bread.

WINTER GREENS *with garlic and almonds*

I absolutely love this side dish and happily have it with some toasted bread for dinner on its own. Actually, you could crumble some feta over the top and serve it on a bed of brown rice or farro as a beautiful vegetarian meal.

SERVES 6

PREP TIME : 10 MINS COOK TIME : 30 MINS

2 heads broccoli
1 bunch kale
1/3 cup (80 ml) olive oil
1 red onion, thinly sliced
6 garlic cloves, finely chopped
1/2 cup (80 g) tamari-roasted almonds or natural almonds, roughly chopped

Preheat the oven to 200°C (400°F). Trim the base of the broccoli heads and cut the florets into pieces, keeping the stem attached (I never understand why people throw that bit out – it's so good!). Shred the kale leaves, discarding the stems.

Heat half of the oil in a frying pan over medium–high heat and add the broccoli. Cook for 5 minutes or until the broccoli is bright green and beginning to char. Transfer the broccoli to a roasting tin.

Return the frying pan to the heat and add the rest of the olive oil. Cook the onion for a few minutes, then add the garlic and cook for another couple of minutes. Add the shredded kale and toss for a few more minutes.

Tip the kale mixture into the roasting tin with the broccoli and pop it into the oven for 10 minutes to cook through. Sprinkle with the almonds and serve warm with the eye fillet.

ROASTED EYE FILLET *with* QUINCE GLAZE
and parsnip and onion purée

I usually make this with a fillet of venison from our own farm here in Orange (if you'd like to do the same, reduce the cooking time to 10 minutes after the browning stage – venison, being such a lean meat, needs a faster cooking time). It's my family's special occasion dish; we have it for birthday dinners or when we want to really showcase the beautiful delicate flavour and tender texture of the meat we produce. I know that venison isn't always easy to source, so here we have a beef fillet from our fantastic local butcher (hello, Michael!), which is also just beautiful.

SERVES 6
PREP TIME : 20 MINS, PLUS 6 HOURS MARINATING ⟩ COOK TIME : 1½ HOURS

800 g (1 lb 12 oz) beef eye fillet	**Parsnip and onion purée**
4 garlic cloves, finely chopped	2 Tbsp (40 g) butter
2 Tbsp thyme leaves	2 brown onions, roughly chopped
3 anchovy fillets	1 kg (2 lb 4 oz) parsnips, peeled and
1/3 cup (80 ml) olive oil	roughly chopped
1 cup (250 ml) white wine	1 tsp sea salt
2 Tbsp quince paste	2 cups (500 ml) chicken or vegetable stock

Put the beef on a large plate. Combine the garlic, thyme, anchovy fillets and 2 tablespoons of the olive oil in a small bowl and mash with a fork to make a rough paste. Rub the paste all over the beef, then loosely wrap with a clean, damp tea towel or plastic wrap and place in the fridge for at least 6 hours or overnight.

For the parsnip and onion purée, heat the butter in a frying pan over medium heat. Cook the onion for about 8 minutes or until completely soft and cooked through. Add the parsnip and salt and cook for another minute or so. Pour in the stock, cover and cook for 25 minutes or until the parsnip is completely tender. Transfer the mixture to a blender or food processor and blitz to a smooth purée. Keep the purée warm until serving, or pop it into the fridge and reheat it when needed.

Preheat the oven to 180°C (350°F). Heat the remaining olive oil in an ovenproof frying pan and brown the beef all over, about 6 minutes on each side or until really well sealed. Put the pan in the oven for 20 minutes or until the beef is cooked to your liking. Transfer the beef to a chopping board, cover with foil and leave to rest for 15 minutes.

While the meat is resting, use the roasting juices to make the rich quince glaze. Put the pan over medium–high heat and pour in the wine. As it bubbles away, scrape up every little bit of flavoursome residue on the bottom of the pan. Once the wine has reduced by half, whisk the quince paste into the glaze. Thin out the glaze with a little water and season to taste. Strain the glaze into a jug and keep warm until serving.

Thinly slice the beef and place it on top of the warm parsnip and onion purée on a serving platter. Drizzle the glaze over the beef just before serving.

CHOCOLATE BARK

Chocolate bark is such a fantastic treat to make and put out for dessert. It's easy, pretty, delicious and requires zero cutlery, plates or extra washing up. Play around with your favourite toppings, but do try to always go with a really good-quality chocolate.

You could also go for a fruit and nut vibe and chop up some beautiful dried figs or apricots and mix in some toasted hazelnuts or almonds. Otherwise, smash up some freeze-dried raspberries or strawberries and scatter them over melted white chocolate.

SERVES 6–8 (WITH WELCOME LEFTOVERS!)
PREP TIME : 10 MINS ⟩ COOK TIME : 10 MINS

Milk chocolate and walnut bark
500 g (1 lb 2 oz) good-quality milk chocolate, chopped
1 cup (140 g) candied walnuts (page 58), roughly chopped

White chocolate and rose bark
500 g (1 lb 2 oz) good-quality white chocolate, chopped
1/3 cup (60 g) pink cachous (or anything else you fancy!)
3 Tbsp dried rose petals

Line two baking trays with baking paper.

For the milk chocolate and walnut bark, melt the chocolate in a heatproof glass bowl sitting over a saucepan of simmering water (don't let the water touch the bowl). Once the chocolate is melted and smooth, spread it over one of the baking trays so you have a thin oval of melted chocolate. Sprinkle the candied walnuts over the chocolate and place in the fridge to set.

For the white chocolate and rose bark, melt and spread the white chocolate using the same method as above, then sprinkle it with the pink cachous and dried rose petals. Place in the fridge to set.

Break the chocolate into shards and serve it in small bowls.

Orange sherbet cocktails

For each person, pour 30 ml (1 fl oz) of Orange sherbet (page 221) into a cocktail glass. Add ice and vodka to taste, then top up with sparkling water. Pop a little rosemary sprig in the glass and finish with a thin strip of orange peel.

In this photo, my son Tom is holding a piece of the 'visitor cake' from page 154 in the one hand and hugging our dog Elton, who sadly has since passed away, with the other. It's one of my favourite photos of all and is framed in the kitchen as a reminder that sometimes being in good company also means being happy in your own. With cake. And preferably the dog.

MENU PLANNER

Casual for a crowd

FRIDAY NIGHT DRINKS
When you've got friends coming over after work and want something to nibble on that will probably end up being dinner.

Salmon rillettes *page 110*
Warm streaky bacon, blue cheese
  and fig bruschetta *page 86*
Olive and hazelnut tapenade and crusty
  bread *page 93*
Amaro spritz *page 186*

GRAZING PLATTER FOR BOOK CLUB
For when you don't want to miss a minute of the conversation.

Olive and hazelnut tapenade *page 93*
Fiona's olive oil crackers and a selection
  of cheeses *page 48*
Tomato, rockmelon and hot-smoked trout
  bruschetta *page 86*
Arancini *page 89*
Praline truffles *page 80*

CHRISTMAS DRINKS WITH THE LOCALS
Love thy neighbours and show them how much by setting out this menu on a trestle table in the lane or on the driveway. Get everyone to bring a plate and catch up properly, not just in passing.

Mezze platter *pages 94–99*
Sticky spiced chicken wings *page 237*
Peach and rosemary G&T *page 93*

NEW YEAR'S DAY LUNCH
We all know that the day after New Year's Eve is the most fun! An easy, delicious spread to serve buffet-style over a long, slow few hours.

Marinated green olives and feta *page 15*
Barbecued lamb shoulder with whipped feta
  and pistachio crumbs *page 25*
Zingy carrot and ginger salad *page 42*
Brown sugar meringue sundaes *pages 240–243*

A shared table

DINNER IN A RUSH
For when you decide to invite everyone back to your place for dinner. It's cool; you've got this.

Amaro spritz *page 186*
Fresh ricotta and tomato pasta *page 113*
Crunchy salad *page 79*
Fresh berries and ice cream

COSY SUPPER
For sharing at the kitchen bench or by the fire. Easy, comforting and delicious.

Polpettone in tomato sauce with greens
  and crusty bread *page 147*
Fennel, parmesan and apple slaw *page 14*
Warm fruit salad with malt crumbs
  and ice cream *page 45*

WOO IS ME
A dinner to knock the socks off your intended or existing love.

Vodka sour cocktails *page 77*
Roasted eye fillet with quince glaze and
  parsnip and onion purée *page 249*
Elderflower and prosecco jellies with cream
  and berries *page 128*

MIDWINTER COMFORT
A dinner to lift spirits on the coldest of days.

Fried chicken with hot honey butter *page 200*
Creamed green curry corn *page 203*
Chocolate bark and orange sherbet
  cocktails *page 250*

Picnic perfection

A PICNIC BASKET FOR A PERFECT SPRING DAY

For when the sun is out, the grass is green and you've got the whole day to pack for, share and then sleep off a picnic.

Fiona's olive oil crackers with cheese and
 pickles *page 48*
Chicken potato salad with salsa verde *page 127*
Orange and honey melt-and-mix cake *page 26*

A THERMOS AND A CAKE FOR SPORTS DAY

The one where you're standing around watching kids sports all day and you want something yummy to help pass the time.

Spicy nutty snacking mix *page 209*
Big flavour tomato soup *page 226*
Hummingbird loaf cake *page 161*

SUMMER EVENING PICNIC

An easy, delicious supper for those golden and warm summer evenings.

Chargrilled zucchini and nasturtium pesto
 bruschetta *page 87*
Greek salad with chicken, risoni and
 caramelised lemon *page 57*
Chocolate, caramel and toasted sesame
 slice *page 233*

WINTER BARBECUE PICNIC

For freezing, bright Saturdays when you can light a fire, cook over it and then spend the afternoon soaking up the winter sunshine.

Pistachio and mint tapenade *page 97*
Zataar-baked pita chips *page 99*
Hamburgers with miso butter and pink
 sauce *page 238*
Ali's toasted coconut marshmallows
 page 221

Tea and sympathy

WORKING BEE SMOKO BREAK

A morning tea with heft – something substantial and sweet to see your helpers through till lunch.

Little herb pies with pickles *page 144*
Ginger crunch bars with custard and
 rhubarb *page 52*
Cinnamon and fruit scones with jam *page 162*

CARE PACKAGE

A few goodies to pop in the post and send via express to a friend in need.

Caramel popcorn with smashed pretzels *page 218*
Rhubarb and vanilla jam *page 157*
Walnut and fennel biscotti *page 151*

DINNER DROP-OFF FOR THE NEW PARENTS

When you want to make dinner that will comfort and nourish, and stretch for visitors and leftovers.

Winter sun soup *page 198*
Baked pasta with fennel sausage *page 136*
Narnie's apple pie *page 230*

MORNING TEA FOR MUM'S BIRTHDAY

For a sunny morning celebration of your mum (or dad or friend or whoever).

Peach, pine nut and lavender cake *page 71*
Rhubarb, orange and pistachio thumbprints
 page 157
Blood orange shrub over ice with mineral
 water *page 221*

CONTRIBUTORS

All at sea (page 20)
Poppy and Rupert Roxburgh of Beachwood
Designs @beachwooddesigns
Live in Bilgola Beach, NSW with sons Oliver,
Henry, Tom and Edward

Keeping the kids happy (page 38)
Clancy Job @clancyjob (photographer)
Lives in Narromine, NSW with husband Matt
and kids Dolly, Daisy, Trader and Hardy

Spring supper picnic (page 46)
Fiona and Adam Walmsley of Buena Vista Farm
@buenavistafarm (dairy goats, cheese, sourdough
workshops)
Live in Gerringong, NSW with kids Henry, Tilly
and Ivy

Bruschetta platter (page 84)
Harriet Goodall @harrietgoodallartist (artist
creating woven lighting and basketry and
hosting retreats)
Lives in Robertson, NSW with husband Mat
and kids Banjo and Clementine

Cheese platter (page 90)
Cressida and Michael Cains from Pecora Dairy
@pecoradairy (cheesemakers/farmers)
Live in Robertson, NSW with sons Hugo and Darcy

A gentle dinner for a hot night (page 106)
Belinda Satterthwaite @tomolly_carcoar
(shopkeeper, curator and stylist)
Lives in Carcoar, NSW with her husband Stephen
and grown-up kids Tom and Molly

Ideas for the big family gathering (page 118)
Annie Herron @artclasseswithannieherron
Lives in Rydal, NSW with husband Henry
(my mum and dad!)

Beating the Sunday night blues (page 134)
Emma Blake @emmablakefloral (florist
extraordinaire!)
Lives in Moss Vale, NSW with husband Gep
and daughters Charlie and Sophia

Passata day at Girragirra (page 140)
Wendy and Kim Muffet @girragirra
(eco-accommodation and sourdough and
fermented food workshops)
Live in Forbes, NSW

The visitor cake (page 152)
Tania Robinson @southernwildco (maker
of Southern Wild Co Candles, designer and
photographer)
Lives in Rocklea, NSW with partner Matt
and puppy Boris

Autumn feast (page 178)
Asia Upward @loganbraeorchard (apples,
events, photography)
Lives in Blackheath, NSW with husband Sam
and daughters Grace and Isla

Loaves and fishes (page 184)
Annabelle Hickson @annabellehickson
(writer, photographer, pecan farmer, publisher
of Galah Press)
Lives in Tenterfield, NSW with husband Ed
and kids Daisy, Tom and Harriet

Ease the bleak midwinter (page 196)
Laura Gardner @_lauraagardner (studying nursing
at university in Sydney)
Lives (part time) in Mittagong, NSW
@pavilioncottages with parents Annie
@_anniethinggoes and Darren and brother Nick

Curry night (page 206)
Kate McKay @kate_mckay_ceramics and
@collector_wines
Lives in Collector, NSW with husband James
and daughters Lucie and Sophie

Wintery ploughman's lunch (page 224)
Em and Ed Swift @printhiewines (makers of
Printhie Wines)
Live in Orange, NSW with daughters Penny
and Annabel

Sunday best (page 244)
Jemima Aldridge and Moir Jones, co-hosts of
@the_repose (beautiful B&B in Dubbo, NSW)
Jemima @jemima.aldridge (creative direction/
experiential spaces) lives in Dubbo, NSW with
partner Bede (@saddlerandco) and their
five sons

ACKNOWLEDGEMENTS

This book is dedicated, with thanks, to all the clever, generous and inspiring people who appear throughout its pages; from my wonderful family, to old friends who are so precious to me and new friends who I am so excited to know, and to be getting to know. I loved cooking for, and with, all of you.

I'd also love to acknowledge and thank the team at Murdoch Books for helping make this book happen, especially to my publisher Corinne Roberts, who always makes the time to offer me such wise advice and guidance. I feel incredibly lucky for the chance to work with you. Thank you also to designer Vivien Valk, for pouring so much love and care into every single page of this book and to editor Justine Harding, for your thoughtful and meticulous work on the copy. What a dream team.

Most of all, this book is dedicated to the people whose company I love best (and my three favourite people to cook for): my husband Tim and our children, Alice and Tom.

The Publisher would like to give especial thanks to Henry and Annie Herron for allowing us to photograph key elements of this book at their beautiful farm on the western side of the Blue Mountains of NSW.

Thank you, Henry and Annie, for your enthusiasm, warmth and hospitality.

artclasseswithannieherron.com.au

INDEX

Published in 2021 by Murdoch Books, an imprint of Allen & Unwin

Murdoch Books Australia
83 Alexander Street
Crows Nest NSW 2065
Phone: +61 (0)2 8425 0100
murdochbooks.com.au
info@murdochbooks.com.au

Murdoch Books UK
Ormond House
26–27 Boswell Street
London WC1N 3JZ
Phone: +44 (0) 20 8785 5995
murdochbooks.co.uk
info@murdochbooks.co.uk

For corporate orders and custom publishing, contact our business development team at
salesenquiries@murdochbooks.com.au

Publisher: Corinne Roberts
Design Manager and Designer: Vivien Valk
Editorial Manager: Virginia Birch
Editor: Justine Harding
Photographer: Sophie Hansen, except page 222 by Annabelle Hickson, and front cover and
pages 2, 3, 6, 29, 34, 35, 257 and 264 by Clancy Job
Production Director: Lou Playfair

The recipes from the Working lunch (pages 54–61) and Sunday best (pages 244–251) menus first
appeared in *Graziher* magazine @graziher.

ISBN 978 1 92235 113 5 Australia
ISBN 978 1 91166 803 9 UK

A catalogue record for this book is available
from the National Library of Australia

A catalogue record for this book is available from the British Library

Colour reproduction by Splitting Image Colour Studio Pty Ltd, Clayton, Victoria
Printed by C & C Offset Printing Co. Ltd., China

TABLESPOON MEASURES: We have used 20 ml (4 teaspoon) tablespoon measures. If you are using
a 15 ml (3 teaspoon) tablespoon add an extra teaspoon of the ingredient for each tablespoon specified.

OVEN GUIDE: You may find cooking times vary depending on the oven you are using. For fan-forced
ovens, as a general rule, set the oven temperature to 20°C (70°F) lower than indicated in the recipe.

10 9 8 7 6 5 4 3 2 1